___ Urvashi,
___ you will read it and appreciate the philosophy.
All my love always and forever —
MAMOO.

7/3/97

To my dear

SRIMAD BHAGAVAD-GITA

TRANSLATION
BY
SWAMI VIRESWARANANDA

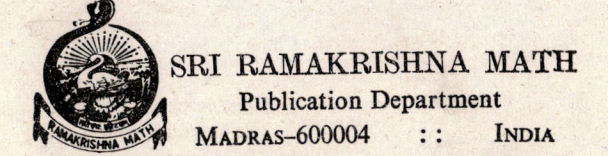

SRI RAMAKRISHNA MATH
Publication Department
MADRAS–600004 :: INDIA

Published by :
© The President,
Sri Ramakrishna Math,
Mylapore, Madras 600 004.

All Rights Reserved
Tenth Impression
X-10M 6C-3-92
ISBN 81-7120-074-5

Printed in India at
Sri Ramakrishna Math Printing Press,
Mylapore, Madras 600 004.

PREFACE

We have great pleasure in bringing out this pocket edition of the Bhagavad Gita with the Text in Devanagari and its translation into English by Swami Vireswarananda. The translation is the same as in Swami Vireswarananda's bigger edition of the Gita with Sridhara's commentary in English. We hope this compact edition of the Gita with a precise but readable English translation will meet the needs of busy men who feel drawn to this famous scriptural text.

PUBLISHER.

CONTENTS

PREFACE	...	iii
INVOCATION	...	vi

CHAPTER

I.	The Despondency of Arjuna	...	1
II.	The Way of Discrimination	...	26
III.	The Way of Action	...	66
IV.	The Way of Knowledge	...	88
V.	Renunciation of Action	...	110
VI.	The Way of Contemplation	...	126
VII.	The Way of Knowledge and Realization	...	149
VIII.	The Way to the Supreme Spirit	...	165
IX.	The Way of Royal Knowledge and Royal Secret	...	180

X.	Meditation on the Divine Glories	198
XI.	The Vision of the Universal Form	220
XII.	The Way of Devotion	249
XIII.	Discrimination Between Nature and Soul.	259
XIV.	The Separation of the Three Gunas	276
XV.	The Way to the Supreme Person	290
XVI.	The Distinction Between Divine and Demoniac attributes	300
XVII.	The Separation of the Three Kinds of Faith	313
XVIII.	The Way of Renunciation	327
	Greatness of the Gita	367

INVOCATION

ॐ पार्थाय प्रतिबोधितां भगवता नारायणेन स्वयं
व्यासेन ग्रथितां पुराणमुनिना मध्ये महाभारतम् ।
अद्वैतामृतवर्षिणीं भगवतीमष्टादशाध्यायिनी-
मम्ब त्वामनुसन्दधामि भगवद्गीते भवद्वेषिणीम् ॥ १ ॥

1. Om! O Bhagavad-Gita with which Pārtba was
enlightened by the Lord Nārāyana Himself and which was
incorporated in the Mahābhārata by the ancient sage
Vyāsa—the blessed Mother, the Destroyer of rebirth,
showering down the nectar of Advaita, and consisting of
eighteen chapters—upon Thee, O Bhagavad-Gita! O loving
Mother! I meditate.

INVOCATION

नमोस्तु ते व्यास विशालबुद्धे फुल्लारविन्दायतपत्रनेत्र ।
येन त्वया भारततैलपूर्णः प्रज्वालितो ज्ञानमयः प्रदीपः ॥ २ ॥

2. Salutation to thee, O Vyāsa, of mighty intellect and with eyes large like the petals of a full-blown lotus, by whom was lighted the lamp of wisdom, full of the Mahābhārata oil.

प्रपन्नपारिजाताय तोत्रवेत्रैकपाणये ।
ज्ञानमुद्राय कृष्णाय गीतामृतदुहे नमः ॥ ३ ॥

3. Salutation to Kṛṣṇa, the holder of *Jnanamudra*, the granter of desires of those who take refuge in Him, the milker of the Gita-nectar, in whose hand is the cane for driving cows.

INVOCATION

सर्वोपनिषदो गावो दोग्धा गोपालनन्दनः ।
पार्थो वत्सः सुधीर्भोक्ता दुग्धं गीतामृतं महत् ॥ ४ ॥

4. All the Upanishads are the cows, the son of the cowherd is the milker, Pārtha is the calf, men of purified intellect are the drinkers and the supreme nectar Gītā is the milk,

वसुदेवसुतं देवं कंसचाणूरमर्दनम् ।
देवकीपरमानन्दं कृष्णं वन्दे जगद्गुरुम् ॥ ५ ॥

5. I salute Kṛṣṇa, the Guru of the Universe, God, the son of Vasudeva, the Destroyer of Kamsa and Cāṇūra, the supreme bliss of Devakī.

युधामन्युश्च विक्रान्त उत्तमौजाश्च वीर्यवान् ।
सौभद्रो दौपदेयाश्च सर्व एव महारथाः ॥ ६ ॥
अस्माकं तु विशिष्टा ये तान्निबोध द्विजोत्तम ।
नायका मम सैन्यस्य संज्ञार्थं तान् ब्रवीमि ते ॥ ७ ॥

6. "Yudhāmanyu the powerful, Uttamaujas the valiant, the son of Subhadrā, and the sons of Draupadi—all mighty warriors (Māharathāh).

7. "Know also, O best amongst the twice-born (Brāhmanas), those who are distinguished amongst us, the leaders of my army. I shall name them for your information.

THE DESPONDENCY OF ARJUNA

अत्र शूरा महेष्वासा भीमार्जुन-समा युधि ।
युयुधानो विराटश्च द्रुपदश्च महारथः ॥ ४ ॥

धृष्टकेतुश्चेकितानः काशिराजश्च वीर्यवान्
पुरुजित्कुन्तिभोजश्च शैब्यश्च नरपुङ्गवः ॥ ५ ॥

4. "Here are mighty-bowed heroes, equals of Bhīma and Arjuna in battle—Yuyudhāna (Sātyaki), and Virāta and Drupada, the mighty warrior.

5. "Dhrishtaketu, Chekitāna, the valiant king of Kāsi, Purujit, Kuntibhoja and that prince amongst men, the king of the Shibis.

सञ्जय उवाच—

दृष्ट्वा तु पाण्डवानीकं व्यूढं दुर्योधनस्तदा ।
आचार्य-मुपसङ्गम्य-राजा वचन-मब्रवीत् ॥ २ ॥
पश्यैतां पाण्डुपुत्राणा-माचार्य महतीं चमूम् ।
व्यूढां द्रुपदपुत्रेण तव शिष्येण धीमता ॥ ३ ॥

Sanjaya said:

2. Having seen the army of the sons of Pāndu arrayed, King Duryodhana then approached the preceptor (Drona), and spoke (these) words:

3. "Behold, O preceptor, this vast army of the Pāndavas arrayed by the son of Drupada, your gifted disciple.

|| प्रथमोऽध्यायः ||

Chapter I

(अर्जुनविषादयोगः)

THE DESPONDENCY OF ARJUNA

धृतराष्ट्र उवाच—

धर्मक्षेत्रे कुरुक्षेत्रे समवेता युयुत्सवः ।
मामकाः पाण्डवाश्चैव किमकुर्वत सञ्जय || १ ||

Dhritarāshtra said:

1. Gathered on the holy plain of Kurukshetra,
O Sanjaya, what did my sons and the sons of Pāndu,
eager to fight, do?

hymns; whom the singers of Sāma sing by the Vedas with their full complement of parts, consecutive sections, and Upaniṣads; whom the Yogis see with their minds absorbed in Him through perfection in meditation; and whose limit the hosts of Devas and Asuras know not.*

---

* The above translation is taken, with the kind permission of the Publisher, from the Mayavati Advaita Ashrama edition of the Bhagavad Gita translated by Swami Swarupananda.

INVOCATION

मूकं करोति वाचालं पङ्गुं लङ्घयते गिरिम् ।
यत्कृपा तमहं वन्दे परमानन्दमाधवम् ॥ ८ ॥

8. I salute that All-bliss Mādhava whose compassion makes the mute eloquent and the cripple cross mountains.

यं ब्रह्मा वरुणेन्द्ररुद्रमरुतः स्तुन्वन्ति दिव्यैः स्तवै-
र्वेदैः साङ्गपदक्रमोपनिषदैर्गायन्ति यं सामगाः ।
ध्यानावस्थिततद्गतेन मनसा पश्यन्ति यं योगिनो
यस्यान्तं न विदुः सुरासुरगणा देवाय तस्मै नमः ॥ ९ ॥

9. Salutation to that God whom the Creator Brahmā, Varuṇa, Indra, Rudra and the Maruts praise with divine

पाराशर्यवचःसरोजममलं गीतार्थगन्धोत्कटं
नानाख्यानककेसरं हरिकथासम्बोधनाबोधितम् ।
लोके सज्जनषट्पदैरहरहः पेपीयमानं मुदा
भूयाद्भारतपङ्कजं कलिमलप्रध्वंसिनः श्रेयसे ॥ ७ ॥

7. May the taintless lotus of the Mahābhārata—growing on the waters of the words of Parāsara's son, having the Gita as its strong sweet fragrance, with many a narrative as its stamens, fully opened by the discourses on Hari and drunk joyously day after day by the Bhramara of the good and the pure in the world—be productive of the supreme good to him who is eager to destroy the taint of Kali!

INVOCATION

भीष्मद्रोणतटा जयद्रथजला गान्धारनीलोत्पला ।
शल्यग्राहवती कृपेण वहनी कर्णेन वेलाकुला ।

अश्वत्थामविकर्णघोरमकरा दुर्योधनावर्तिनी ।
सोत्तीर्णा खलु पाण्डवैरणनदी कैवर्तकः केशवः ॥ ६ ॥

6. The battle river with Bhīṣma and Droṇa as its
banks and Jayadratha as the water, with the king of
Gāndhāra as the blue water-lily and Salya as the shark,
with Kṛpa as the current and Karṇa as the breakers, with
Asvatthāma and Vikarṇa as terrible Makaras and Duryodhana as the whirlpool in it—was indeed crossed over by
the Pāṇḍavas, with Kesava as the ferryman.

भवान् भीष्मश्च कर्णश्च कृपश्च समितिञ्जयः ।
अश्वत्थामा विकर्णश्च सौमदत्तिस्तथैव च ॥ ८ ॥

अन्ये च बहवः शूरा मदर्थे त्यक्तजीविताः ।
नानाशस्त्र-प्रहरणाः सर्वे युद्ध-विशारदाः ॥ ९ ॥

8. "Yourself, Bhishma, Karna and Kripa, the winner of battles; Asvatthāma, Vikarna and also the son of Somadatta.

9. "And many other heroes as well are there, determined to give up their lives for my sake, wielding various (kinds of) weapons for attack, all dexterous in battle.

अपर्याप्तं तदस्माकं बलं भीष्माभिरक्षितम् ।
पर्याप्तं त्विदमेतेषां बलं भीमाभिरक्षितम् ॥ १० ॥
अयनेषु च सर्वेषु यथाभाग-मवस्थिताः ।
भीष्म-मेवाभिरक्षन्तु भवन्तः सर्व एव हि ॥ ११ ॥

10. "That army of ours, protected by Bhīshma, is insufficient; but this army of theirs, protected by Bhīma is sufficient.

11. "(Therefore) do you all, keeping to your respective stations, at all approaches to the army, protect Bhīshma alone on all sides".

तस्य सञ्जनयन् हर्षं कुरुवृद्धः पितामहः ।
सिंहनादं विनद्योच्चैः शङ्खं दध्मौ प्रतापवान् ॥ १२ ॥

ततः शङ्खाश्च भेर्यश्च पणवानक-गोमुखाः ।
सहसैवाभ्यहन्यन्त स शब्दस्तुमुलोऽभवत् ॥ १३ ॥

12. Gladdening his (Duryodhana's) heart, the powerful eldest of the Kurus, the grandsire, thundered forth a lion's roar, and blew his conch.

13. Then, all of a sudden conchs, kettle-drums, trumpets, drums, and horns blared forth; that sound was tumultuous.

ततः श्वेतै-र्हयैर्युक्ते महति स्यन्दने स्थितौ ।
माधवः पाण्डवश्चैव दिव्यौ शङ्खौ प्रदध्मतुः ॥ १४ ॥

पाञ्चजन्यं हृषीकेशो देवदत्तं धनञ्जयः ।
पौण्ड्रं दध्मौ महाशङ्खं भीमकर्मा वृकोदरः ॥ १५ ॥

14. Then, seated in a great chariot to which white horses were yoked, Mādhava (Sri Krishna) and Pāndava (Arjuna) blew their celestial conchs.

15. Hrishikesa (Krishna) blew the (conch) Pānchajanya Dhananjaya (Arjuna) the Devadatta, and Vrikodara (Bhīma) of terrible deeds blew the great conch Paundra.

अनन्तविजयं राजा कुन्तीपुत्रो युधिष्ठिरः ।
नकुलः सहदेवश्च सुघोष-मणिपुष्पकौ ॥ १६ ॥

काश्यश्च परमेष्वासः शिखण्डी च महारथः ।
धृष्टद्युम्नो विराटश्च सात्यकिश्चापराजितः ॥ १७ ॥

16. King Yudhishthira, the son of Kunti, blew the Anantavijaya and Nakula and Sahadeva, the Sughosha and Manipushpaka respectively.

17-18. The Mighty-bowed king of Kāsi, the mighty warrior Sikhandi, Dhrishtadyumna, Virāta, the unconquered Sātyaki, Drupada, the sons of Draupadi, and Subhadrā's son

SRIMAD-BHAGAVAD-GITA

द्रुपदो द्रौपदेयाश्च सर्वशः पृथिवीपते ।
सौभद्रश्च महाबाहुः शङ्खान्दध्मुः पृथक् पृथक् ॥ १८ ॥

स घोषो धार्तराष्ट्राणां हृदयानि व्यदारयत् ।
नभश्च पृथिवीं चैव तुमुलो व्यनुनादयन् ॥ १९ ॥

of powerful arms, (all), O Lord of the earth, blew their
respective conchs on all sides.

19. That great tumult, making the heaven and earth
resound, rent the hearts of Dhritarāshtra's sons.

THE DESPONDENCY OF ARJUNA

अथ व्यवस्थितान्दृष्ट्वा धार्तराष्ट्रान् कपिध्वजः ।
प्रवृत्ते शस्त्रसंपाते धनुरुद्यम्य पाण्डवः ॥ २० ॥

हृषीकेशं तदा वाक्यमिदमाह महीपते ।

20-22. Then the monkey-bannered son of Pāndu, (Arjuna) when he saw the sons of Dhritarāshtra (thus) arrayed, and when missiles were about to be discharged, raised his bow, O king, and said to Hrishikesa (Sri Krishna) the following words:

SRIMAD-BHAGAVAD-GITA

अर्जुन उवाच—

सेनयोरुभयोर्मध्ये रथं स्थापय मेऽच्युत ॥ २१ ॥

यावदेतान्निरीक्षेऽहं योद्धुकामा-नवस्थितान् ।
कैर्मया सह योद्धव्य-मस्मिन् रणसमुद्यमे ॥ २२ ॥

Arjuna said :

O Achyuta, (Sri Krishna) keep my chariot between the two armies while I see those who are arrayed, seeking battle, and know with whom I shall have to fight in this preparation for combat.

THE DESPONDENCY OF ARJUNA

योत्स्यमाना-नवेक्षेऽहं य एतेऽत्र समागताः ।
धार्तराष्ट्रस्य दुर्बुद्धे-र्युद्धे प्रियचिकीर्षवः ॥ २३ ॥

सञ्जय उवाच—
एवमुक्तो हृषीकेशो गुडाकेशेन भारत ।
सेनयोरुभयोर्मध्ये स्थापयित्वा रथोत्तमम् ॥ २४ ॥

23. (And while) I see those who are gathered here ready for fight, desirous of pleasing in battle the evil-minded son of Dhritarāshtra.

Sanjaya said:

24-25. O descendant of Bharata (Dhritarāshtra), thus spoken to by Gudākesa (Arjuna), Hrishīkesa (Sri Krishna),

SRIMAD-BHAGAVAD-GITA

भीष्म-द्रोण-प्रमुखतः सर्वेषां च महीक्षिताम् ।
उवाच पार्थ पश्यैतान् समवेतान् कुरूनिति ॥ २५ ॥
तत्रापश्यत्स्थितान्पार्थः पितृनथ पितामहान् ।
आचार्यान् मातुलान् भ्रातृन् पुत्रान् पौत्रान् सखींस्तथा ॥२६॥

placing that excellent chariot between the two armies, in front of Bhīshma, Drona, and all the kings, said, "See, O son of Prithā (Arjuna), these assembled Kurus."

26. There, situated in both the armies, Pārtha (Arjuna) saw fathers, as also grandsires, preceptors, maternal uncles, brothers, sons, grandsons, associates, fathers-in-law, and well-wishers.

श्वशुरान् सुहृदश्चैव सेनयोरुभयोरपि ।
तान् समीक्ष्य स कौन्तेयः सर्वान् बन्धू-नवस्थितान् ॥ २७ ॥

कृपया परयाऽऽविष्टो विषीद-न्निदमब्रवीत् ।

अर्जुन उवाच—

दृष्ट्वेमं स्वजनं कृष्ण युयुत्सुं समुपस्थितम् ॥ २८ ॥

27. Seeing all these kinsmen gathered together, the son of Kunti, overcome with great compassion, spoke thus in grief.

Arjuna said:

28. Seeing these kinsmen, O Krishna, arrayed with a view to fighting, my limbs fail, and my mouth is parched up.

SRIMAD-BHAGAVAD-GITA

सीदन्ति मम गात्राणि मुखं च परिशुष्यति ।
वेपथुश्च शरीरे मे रोमहर्षश्च जायते ॥ २९ ॥

गाण्डीवं स्रंसते हस्तात्त्वक्चैव परिदह्यते ।
न च शक्नोम्यवस्थातुं भ्रमतीव च मे मनः ॥ ३० ॥

29. My body quivers, and there is horripilation ; the Gāndiva (Arjuna's bow) slips from my hands, and my skin burns.

30. I am not able to stand, my mind is reeling, as it were, and I see, O Keshava (Sri Krishna), adverse omens.

निमित्तानि च पश्यामि विपरीतानि केशव ।
न च श्रेयोऽनुपश्यामि हत्वा स्वजन-माहवे ॥ ३१ ॥
न काङ्क्षे विजयं कृष्ण न च राज्यं सुखानि च ।
किं नो राज्येन गोविन्द किं भोगै-र्जीवितेन वा ॥ ३२ ॥

31-32. And I see no good from killing kinsmen in battle. I do not desire victory, O Krishna, nor sovereignty, nor pleasures; of what use is sovereignty to us, O Govinda (Sri Krishna), or enjoyments, or life itself?

येषामर्थे काङ्क्षितं नो राज्यं भोगाः सुखानि च ।
त इमेऽवस्थिता युद्धे प्राणांस्त्यक्त्वा धनानि च ॥ ३३ ॥
आचार्याः पितरः पुत्रास्तथैव च पितामहाः ।
मातुलाः श्वशुराः पौत्राः स्यालाः संबन्धिन-स्तथा ॥ ३४ ॥

33. They for whose sake we desire sovereignty, enjoyments and pleasures, are gathered here for battle, giving up (their) lives and wealth.

34. Preceptors, fathers, sons, as also grandsires; maternal uncles, fathers-in-law, grandsons, brothers-in-law, and other kinsmen as well.

एतान्न हन्तुमिच्छामि घ्नतोऽपि मधुसूदन ।
अपि त्रैलोक्य-राज्यस्य हेतोः किं नु महीकृते ॥ ३५ ॥
निहत्य धार्तराष्ट्रान्नः का प्रीतिः स्याज्जनार्दन ।
पापमेवाश्रये-दस्मान् हत्वैता-नाततायिनः ॥ ३६ ॥

35. I do not like to kill them, O Madhusūdana (Sri Krishna), even if they should kill us, no, not even for the sovereignty of the three worlds, much less for that of this earth.

36. What joy will be ours, O Janārdana (Sri Krishna), by slaying these sons of Dhritarāshtra? Sin alone will overtake us if we kill these aggressors.

SRIMAD-BHAGAVAD-GITA

तस्मान्नार्हा वयं हन्तुं धार्तराष्ट्रान् स्वबान्धवान् ।
स्वजनं हि कथं हत्वा सुखिनः स्याम माधव ॥ ३७ ॥

यद्यप्येते न पश्यन्ति लोभोपहत-चेतसः ।
कुलक्षयकृतं दोषं मित्रद्रोहे च पातकम् ॥ ३८ ॥

37. Therefore we ought not to kill these sons of Dhritarāshtra, our kinsmen; how can we indeed be happy, O Mādhava (Sri Krishna), by killing our own people?

38-39. Although these, with their minds overcome by greed, see no evil in destroying the family or sin in hostility

THE DESPONDENCY OF ARJUNA

कथं न ज्ञेय-मस्माभिः पापा-दस्मा-न्निवर्तितुम् ।
कुलक्षयकृतं दोषं प्रपश्यद्भि-र्जनार्दन ॥ ३९ ॥

कुलक्षये प्रणश्यन्ति कुलधर्माः सनातनाः ।
धर्मे नष्टे कुलं कृत्स्न-मधर्मोऽभिभवत्युत ॥ ४० ॥

to friends, why should we, O Janārdana, who see the evil resulting from destruction of the family, not learn to desist from this sin?

40. With the destruction of the family the time-honoured family traditions are lost; and when the traditions are lost, unrighteousness overtakes the whole family.

अधर्माभिभवात् कृष्ण प्रदुष्यन्ति कुलस्त्रियः ।
स्त्रीषु दुष्टासु वार्ष्णेय जायते वर्णसङ्करः ॥ ४१ ॥

सङ्करो नरकायैव कुलघ्नानां कुलस्य च ।
पतन्ति पितरो ह्येषां लुप्त-पिण्डोदक-क्रियाः ॥ ४२ ॥

41. When unrighteousness prevails, O Krishna, the women of the family become corrupt, and when the women are corrupt, O descendant of the Vrishnis (Krishna), there arises a mixture of castes.

42. The mixture of castes in the family only leads its destroyers to hell; their ancestors fall (from heaven), for they are deprived of the offerings of funeral cakes and drink.

दोषैरेतैः कुलघ्नानां वर्णसङ्कर-कारकैः ।
उत्साद्यन्ते जातिधर्माः कुलधर्माश्च शाश्वताः ॥ ४३ ॥

उत्सन्न-कुलधर्माणां मनुष्याणां जनार्दन ।
नरके नियतं वासो भवतीत्यनुशुश्रुम ॥ ४४ ॥

43. From these sins of the destroyers of the family that lead to a mixture of castes, the long-standing traditions of the caste, the family, etc., are destroyed.

44. Persons whose family traditions are destroyed, O Janārdana, are doomed to live perpetually in hell; thus have we heard.

SRIMAD-BHAGAVAD-GITA

अहो बत महत्पापं कर्तुं व्यवसिता वयम् ।
यद्राज्य-सुखलोभेन हन्तुं स्वजन-मुद्यताः ॥ ४५ ॥

यदि मामप्रतीकार-मशस्त्रं शस्त्रपाणयः ।
धार्तराष्ट्रा रणे हन्यु-स्तन्मे क्षेमतरं भवेत् ॥ ४६ ॥

45. Alas, what a heinous sins we are resolved to commit, in that we are ready to kill our kinsmen, out of greed for the joys of sovereignty.

46. If the sons of Dhritarāshtra with weapons in (tl.eir) hands should slay me in battle, while I am unarmed and unresisting, that would be better for me.

THE DESPONDENCY OF ARJUNA

सञ्जय उवाच—

एवमुक्त्वाऽर्जुनः संख्ये रथोपस्थ उपाविशत् ।
विसृज्य सशरं चापं शोक-संविग्न-मानसः ॥ ४७ ॥

इति श्रीमद्भगवद्गीतासूपनिषत्सु ब्रह्मविद्यायां योगशास्त्रे
श्रीकृष्णार्जुनसंवादेऽर्जुनविषादयोगो नाम
प्रथमोऽध्यायः ॥

Sanjaya said:

47. Thus speaking, Arjuna sat down on the chariot in (that) battle, casting away (his) bow and arrows, being grief-stricken at heart.

॥ द्वितीयोऽध्यायः ॥

Chapter II

(साङ्ख्ययोगः)

THE WAY OF DISCRIMINATION

सञ्जय उवाच—

तं तथा कृपयाऽऽविष्ट-मश्रुपूर्णाकुलेक्षणम् ।
विषीदन्त-मिदं वाक्य-मुवाच मधुसूदनः ॥ १ ॥

Sanjaya said :

1. To him thus overcome with pity and grieving, with eyes filled with tears and agitated, Madhusūdana spoke these words :

THE WAY OF DISCRIMINATION

श्रीभगवानुवाच—
कुतस्त्वा कश्मलमिदं विषमे समुपस्थितम् ।
अनार्यजुष्टमस्वर्ग्यमकीर्तिकरमर्जुन ॥ २ ॥
क्लैब्यं मा स्म गमः पार्थ नैतत्त्वय्युपपद्यते ।
क्षुद्रं हृदयदौर्बल्यं त्यक्त्वोत्तिष्ठ परन्तप ॥ ३ ॥

The Blessed Lord said:

2. Whence, O Arjuna, has this weakness, not entertained by honourable men (Aryans), nor conducive to (the attainment of) heaven, and leading to ill-fame, come on you at this crisis?

3. Yield not to unmanliness, O Pārtha, it is not worthy of you; shaking off this mean faint-heartedness, arise, O scorcher of foes.

अर्जुन उवाच—

कथं भीष्म-महं सङ्ख्ये द्रोणं च मधुसूदन ।
इषुभिः प्रतियोत्स्यामि पूजार्हावरिसूदन ॥ ४ ॥

Arjuna said :

4. How, O Madhusūdana, shall I in battle fight with arrows against Bhīshma and Drona, who are worthy of respect, O slayer of enemies?

गुरू-नहत्वा हि महानुभावान्
श्रेयो भोक्तुं भैक्ष्य-मपीह लोके ।
हत्वाऽर्थकामांस्तु गुरू-निहैव
भुञ्जीय भोगान् रुधिरप्रदिग्धान् ॥ ५ ॥

5. Without killing the noble-minded elders, even to live on alms in the world would be much better. But by killing these elders, I shall be enjoying even here pleasures like wealth and fulfilment of desires, drenched with (their) blood.

SRIMAD-BHAGAVAD-GITA

न चैतद्विद्यः कतरन्नो गरीयो
यद्वा जयेम यदि वा नो जयेयुः ।
यानेव हत्वा न जिजीविषाम-
स्तेऽवस्थिताः प्रमुखे धार्तराष्ट्राः ॥ ६ ॥

6. And we do not know which would be the better course for us—whether we should conquer them or they should conquer us. Those very persons, killing whom we should not desire to live, viz., the sons of Dhritarāshtra, are gathered in front.

कार्पण्यदोषोपहतस्वभावः
पृच्छामि त्वां धर्मसम्मूढचेताः ।
यच्छ्रेयः स्यान्निश्चितं ब्रूहि तन्मे
शिष्यस्तेऽहं शाधि मां त्वां प्रपन्नम् ॥ ७ ॥

7. With my natural traits overcome by (a sense of) helplessness and sin, and my mind perplexed regarding (my) duty, I ask You—tell me that which is definitely good for me. I am Your disciple; teach me who have taken refuge in You.

न हि प्रपश्यामि ममापनुद्याद् यच्छोक-मुच्छोषण-मिन्द्रियाणाम् ।
अवाप्य भूमावसपत्नमृद्धं राज्यं सुराणामपि चाधिपत्यम् ॥ ८ ॥

सञ्जय उवाच—

एवमुक्त्वा हृषीकेशं गुडाकेशः परन्तपः ।
न योत्स्य इति गोविन्द-मुक्त्वा तूष्णीं बभूव ह ॥ ९ ॥

8. I do not indeed see that which would remove this grief of mine that is utterly drying up my senses, even if I were to attain in this world a kingdom without rivals and prosperous, and even lordship over the gods.

Sanjaya said :

9. Having thus spoken to Hrishīkesa, Gudākesa (Arjuna), the harasser of foes, said to Govinda, 'I shall not fight,' and kept quiet.

तमुवाच हृषीकेशः प्रहसन्निव भारत ।
सेनयो-रुभयो-र्मध्ये विषीदन्त मिदं वचः ॥ १० ॥

श्रीभगवानुवाच –

अशोच्या-नन्वशोचस्त्वं प्रज्ञावादांश्च भाषसे ।
गतासू-नगतासूंश्च नानुशोचन्ति पण्डिताः ॥ ११ ॥

10. O descendant of (King) Bharata (Dhritarāshtra), to him who was sorrowing between the two armies, Hrishikesa spoke these words, as if smiling.

The Blessed Lord said:

11. You have been sorrowing for those who should not be grieved for, and (yet) you are talking learned words. The learned grieve neither for the dead nor for the living.

B—2

SRIMAD BHAGAVAD-GITA

न त्वेवाहं जातु नासं न त्वं नेमे जनाधिपाः ।
न चैव न भविष्यामः सर्वे वयमतः परम् ॥ १२ ॥

देहिनोऽस्मिन् यथा देहे कौमारं यौवनं जरा ।
तथा देहान्तरप्राप्ति-र्धीरस्तत्र न मुह्यति ॥ १३ ॥

12. It is not indeed that I did not exist at any time, nor you, nor these kings; nor that we all shall not exist hereafter.

13. Even as the embodied self attains in this body childhood, youth, and old age, so does it attain another body; the wise man does not get deluded at this.

मात्रास्पर्शास्तु कौन्तेय शीतोष्ण-सुखदुःखदाः ।
आगमापायिनोऽनित्यास्तांस्तितिक्षस्व भारत ॥ १४ ॥

यं हि न व्यथयन्त्येते पुरुषं पुरुषर्षभ ।
समदुःखसुखं धीरं सोऽमृतत्वाय कल्पते ॥ १५ ॥

14. O son of Kunti, sense-contacts (with objects) result in heat and cold, pleasure and pain. They are subject to coming and going and are transient; (therefore), O descendant of Bharata (Arjuna), (just) endure them.

15. O best of men, that wise person whom these do not afflict, who is equanimous in pleasure and pain, is fit for immortality.

SRIMAD-BHAGAVAD-GITA

नासतो विद्यते भावो नाभावो विद्यते सतः ।
उभयोरपि दृष्टोऽन्त-स्त्वनयो-स्तत्त्वदर्शिभिः ॥ १६ ॥

अविनाशि तु तद्विद्धि येन सर्व-मिदं ततम् ।
विनाश-मव्ययस्यास्य न कश्चित् कर्तुमर्हति ॥ १७ ॥

16. The unreal has no existence, and the real has no non-existence; the conclusion about both these has been seen by the knowers of Truth.

17. But know that by which all this is pervaded to be imperishable. No one can bring about the destruction of this immutable principle.

अन्तवन्त इमे देहा नित्यस्योक्ताः शरीरिणः ।
अनाशिनोऽप्रमेयस्य तस्माद्युध्यस्व भारत ॥ १८ ॥

य एनं वेत्ति हन्तारं यश्चैनं मन्यते हतम् ।
उभौ तौ न विजानीतो नायं हन्ति न हन्यते ॥ १९ ॥

18. These bodies of the eternal, imperishable, immeasurable, embodied self are said to have an end; therefore, fight, O descendant of Bharata.

19. He who thinks it (self) to be a slayer and he who thinks it is slain, both are ignorant (of the truth); it (self) neither slays nor is slain.

SRIMAD-BHAGAVAD-GITA

न जायते म्रियते वा कदाचिन्नायं भूत्वा भविता वा न भूयः ।
अजो नित्यः शाश्वतोऽयं पुराणो न हन्यते हन्यमाने शरीरे ॥२०॥

वेदाऽविनाशिनं नित्यं य एनमजमव्ययम् ।
कथं स पुरुषः पार्थ कं घातयति हन्ति कम् ॥ २१ ॥

20.   It (self) is not born and it does not die at any time.
And it does not again come into existence by being born.
It (self) is birthless, constant, eternal and ancient; it is not
slain when the body is slain.

21.   Whom, O Pārtha. can that person who knows this
(self) to be imperishable, constant, birthless and immutable
slay or cause to be slain, and how?

वासांसि जीर्णानि यथा विहाय नवानि गृह्णाति नरोऽपराणि ।
तथा शरीराणि विहाय जीर्णान्यन्यानि संयाति नवानि देही ॥

नैनं छिन्दन्ति शस्त्राणि नैनं दहति पावकः ।
न चैनं क्लेदयन्त्यापो न शोषयति मारुतः ॥ २३ ॥

22. Just as a person gives up worn out clothes and puts on other new ones, even so does the embodied self give up decrepit bodies and enter other new ones.

23. Weapons do not cut it, fire does not burn it, water also does not moisten it, and wind does not dry it.

SRIMAD-BHAGAVAD-GITA

अच्छेद्योऽय-मदाह्योऽय-मक्लेद्योऽशोष्य एव च ।
नित्यः सर्वगतः स्थाणु-रचलोऽयं सनातनः ॥ २४ ॥

अव्यक्तोऽय-मचिन्त्योऽय-मविकार्योऽय-मुच्यते ।
तस्मादेवं विदित्वैनं नानुशोचितु-महर्सि ॥ २५ ॥

24. This (self) is indeed incapable of being cut,
of being burnt of being moistened and of being dried; it is
eternal, all-pervading, stable, immovable, and primordial.

25. This (self) is said to be unmanifest, unthinkable,
and unchangeable; therefore, knowing it to be such, you
ought not to grieve.

अथ चैनं नित्यजातं नित्यं वा मन्यसे मृतम् ।
तथापि त्वं महाबाहो नैनं शोचितु-महिस ॥ २६ ॥

जातस्य हि ध्रुवो मृत्युर्ध्रुवं जन्म मृतस्य च ।
तस्मा-दपरिहार्यऽर्थे न त्वं शोचितु-महिस ॥ २७ ॥

26. If, however, you think that it (self) is perpetually born and perpetually dies, even then, O mighty-armed one, you ought not to grieve for it.

27. For to one who is born, death is certain, and to one who dies, rebirth is certain. Therefore over this inevitable fact you ought not to grieve.

SRIMAD-BHAGAVAD-GITA

अव्यक्तादीनि भूतानि व्यक्त-मध्यानि भारत ।
अव्यक्त-निधनान्येव तत्र का परिदेवना ॥ २८ ॥

आश्चर्यवत्पश्यति कश्चिदेनं आश्चर्यवद्वदति तथैव चान्यः ।
आश्चर्यवच्चैन-मन्यः शृणोति श्रुत्वाप्येनं वेद न चैव कश्चित् ॥२९॥

28. Beings, O descendant of Bharata, have the Unmanifest as their beginning, are manifest in the middle, and have their dissolution in the Unmanifest itself; so why lament for them?

29. One sees this (self) as a wonder, so also another talks of this as a wonder, still another hears of this as a wonder, and some other, again, does not know this even after hearing, etc., about it.

देही नित्य-मवध्योऽयं देहे सर्वस्य भारत ।
तस्मात् सर्वाणि भूतानि न त्वं शोचितु-महंसि ॥ ३० ॥

स्वधर्ममपि चावेक्ष्य न विकम्पितु-महंसि ।
धर्म्याद्धि युद्धाच्छ्रेयोऽन्यत् क्षत्रियस्य न विद्यते ॥ ३१ ॥

30. This embodied self in everyone's body is eternally indestructble, O descendant of Bharata (Arjuna); therefore, you ought not to grieve for any creature.

31. And considering your duty also you ought not to falter, because there is no greater good-fortune for a Kshatriya than a righteous battle.

यदृच्छया चोपपन्नं स्वर्गद्वार-मपावृतम् ।
सुखिनः क्षत्रियाः पार्थ लभन्ते युद्ध-मीदृशम् ॥ ३२ ॥

अथ चेत्त्वमिमं धर्म्यं संग्रामं न करिष्यसि ।
ततः स्वधर्मं कीर्तिंश्च हित्वा पाप-मवाप्स्यसि ॥ ३३ ॥

32. And happy, O Pārtha, are the Kshatriyas who get such a battle, which has come of its own accord, and is an open gateway to heaven.

33. If, however, you do not fight this righteous battle, then failing in your duty and losing your reputation, you will incur sin.

अकीर्तिंश्चापि भूतानि कथयिष्यन्ति तेऽव्ययाम् ।
संभावितस्य चाकीर्ति-र्मरणा-दतिरिच्यते ॥ ३४ ॥

भयाद्रणा-दुपरतं मंस्यन्ते त्वां महारथाः ।
येषां च त्वं बहुमतो भूत्वा यास्यसि लाघवम् ॥ ३५ ॥

34. Besides, people will talk of your eternal infamy; and for one held in esteem infamy is worse than death.

35. (These) mighty warriors will think that you have retired from battle through fear. Having been highly esteemed by them, you will (now) fall into disgrace.

SRIMAD-BHAGAVAD-GITA

अवाच्य-वादांश्च बहून् वदिष्यन्ति तवाहिताः ।
निन्दन्तस्तव सामर्थ्यं ततो दुःखतरं नु किम् ॥ ३६ ॥

हतो वा प्राप्स्यसि स्वर्गं जित्वा वा भोक्ष्यसे महीम् ।
तस्मा-दुत्तिष्ठ कौन्तेय युद्धाय कृतनिश्चयः ॥ ३७ ॥

36. And your enemies will be saying many unmention-
able things, decrying your prowess. What can be more
painful than that?

37. Either, killed (in battle), you will attain heaven,
or, being victorious, you will enjoy the earth. Therefore
arise, O son of Kunti, resolved to fight.

सुखदुःखे समे कृत्वा लाभालाभौ जयाजयौ ।
ततो युद्धाय युज्यस्व नैवं पाप-मवाप्स्यसि ॥ ३८ ॥
एषा तेऽभिहिता सांख्ये बुद्धिर्योगे त्विमां शृणु ।
बुद्ध्या युक्तो यया पार्थ कर्मबन्धं प्रहास्यसि ॥ ३९ ॥

38. Regarding pleasure and pain, gain and loss, victory and defeat, as alike, prepare yourself then for battle; you will not thus incur sin.

39. The (requisite) mental attitude towards the Self has just been taught to you, now hear about it in respect of the way of action (Karma-Yoga), being endowed with which (attitude), O Pārtha, you will get rid of the bondage of actions.

नेहाभिक्रम-नाशोऽस्ति प्रत्यवायो न विद्यते ।
स्वल्पमप्यस्य धर्मस्य त्रायते महतो भयात् ॥ ४० ॥

व्यवसायात्मिका बुद्धि-रेकेह कुरुनन्दन ।
बहुशाखा ह्यनन्ताश्च बुद्धयोऽव्यवसायिनाम् ॥ ४१ ॥

40. In this there is no waste of any undertaking nor chance of incurring sin : even the least bit of this religion saves one from great danger.

41. In this, descendant of Kuru, there is a single one-pointed determination. The thoughts of the irresolute are many-branched and infinite.

यामिमां पुष्पितां वाचं प्रवदन्त्यविपश्चितः ।
वेदवादरताः पार्थ नान्यदस्तीति-वादिनः ॥ ४२ ॥

कामात्मानः स्वर्गपरा जन्मकर्म-फलप्रदाम् ।
क्रियाविशेष-बहुलां भोगैश्वर्यगतिं प्रति ॥ ४३ ॥

42-44. The dull-witted, whose minds are full of desires, who regard heaven as their highest goal, who are enamoured of the panegyric statements in the Vedas and assert that there is nothing else (higher than this), speak familiar flowery words about numerous kinds of rites (prescribed by the Vedas) producing birth, actions and their results, as the means to enjoyment and power. Those who are attached

भोगैश्वर्य-प्रसक्तानां तयापहृत-चेतसाम् ।
व्यवसायात्मिका बुद्धिः समाधौ न विधीयते ॥ ४४ ॥

त्रैगुण्य-विषया वेदा निस्त्रैगुण्यो भवार्जुन ।
निर्द्वन्द्वो नित्य-सत्त्वस्थो निर्योगक्षेम आत्मवान् ॥४५॥

to enjoyment and power, and whose minds are carried away
by these (flowery words) do not attain one-pointed determination leading to concentration on the Lord.

45.   The Vedas deal with subjects coming under the three
Gunas. O Arjuna, be above the three Gunas, free from the
dualities, always established in goodness (Sattva), regardless
of acquisition or preservation, and self-possessed.

यावानर्थ उदपाने सर्वतः संप्लुतोदके ।
तावान् सर्वेषु वेदेषु ब्राह्मणस्य विजानतः ॥ ४६ ॥

कर्मण्येवाधिकारस्ते मा फलेषु कदाचन ।
मा कर्मफलहेतुर्भूर्मा ते सङ्गोऽस्त्वकर्मणि ॥ ४७ ॥

46. All the purpose that small reservoirs serve, is served by a vast lake entirely filled with water. Similarly the purpose that all the Vedas serve is attained by a man of realization.

47. To work alone you have the right, but never claim its results. Let not the results of actions be your motive, nor be attached to inaction.

SRIMAD-BHAGAVAD-GITA

योगस्थः कुरु कर्माणि सङ्गं त्यक्त्वा धनञ्जय ।
सिद्ध्यसिद्ध्योः समो भूत्वा समत्वं योग उच्यते ॥ ४८ ॥

दूरेण ह्यवरं कर्म बुद्धियोगा-द्धनञ्जय ।
बुद्धौ शरणमन्विच्छ कृपणाः फलहेतवः ॥ ४९ ॥

48. Established in Yoga, O Dhananjaya (Arjuna), perform actions, giving up attachment, and unconcerned as to success or failure : this equanimity is called Yoga.

49. Far inferior is work (prompted by desire) to work done through wisdom, O Dhanajaya. Take refuge in wisdom : those who are impelled by results are miserable.

बुद्धियुक्तो जहातीह उभे सुकृतदुष्कृते ।
तस्मा-द्योगाय युज्यस्व योगः कर्मसु कौशलम् ॥५०॥

कर्मजं बुद्धियुक्ता हि फलं त्यक्त्वा मनीषिणः ।
जन्मबन्ध-विनिर्मुक्ताः पदं गच्छन्त्यनामयम् ॥५१॥

50. Endowed with this wisdom, one gets rid of both good and evil (even) here; therefore take to Yoga; Yoga is the skill in work.

51. Endowed with wisdom, giving up the fruit resulting from action, attaining self-realization, and freed from the bondage of birth, verily, they go to that abode which is free from evil.

SRIMAD-BHAGAVAD-GITA

यदा ते मोहकलिलं बुद्धि-र्व्यतितरिष्यति ।
तदा गन्तासि निर्वेदं श्रोतव्यस्य श्रुतस्य च ॥ ५२ ॥

श्रुति-विप्रतिपन्ना ते यदा स्थास्यति निश्चला ।
समाधावचला बुद्धिस्तदा योग-मवाप्स्यसि ॥ ५३ ॥

52. When your understanding will get beyond the maze of delusion, then you will have attained the indifference to what is to be heard and what is heard.

53. When your understanding (now) perplexed by hearing will rest in Samādhi (the Lord), unwavering and steady, then you shall attain Yōga.

अर्जुन उवाच—

स्थितप्रज्ञस्य का भाषा समाधिस्थस्य केशव ।
स्थितधीः किं प्रभाषेत किमासीत व्रजेत किम् ॥५४॥

Arjuna said:

54. What is the definition, O Kesava (Krishna), of a man of steady wisdom, absorbed in contemplation? How does a man of steady wisdom talk, how does he sit and how does he walk?

SRIMAD-BHAGAVAD-GITA

श्रीभगवानुवाच—

प्रजहाति यदा कामान् सर्वान् पार्थ मनोगतान् ।
आत्मन्येवात्मना तुष्टः स्थितप्रज्ञ-स्तदोच्यते ॥५५॥

Sri Bhagavan said :

55. When a man gives up all desires of the mind, O
Pārtha, and himself delights in his Self, then he is said to
be a 'a man of steady wisdom.

दुःखेष्वनुद्विग्नमनाः सुखेषु विगतस्पृहः ।
वीतरागभयक्रोधः स्थितधी-र्मुनिरुच्यते ॥ ५६ ॥

यः सर्वत्रानभिस्नेह-स्तत्तत्प्राप्य शुभाशुभम् ।
नाभिनन्दति न द्वेष्टि तस्य प्रज्ञा प्रतिष्ठिता ॥ ५७ ॥

56. He who is unperturbed in misery and free from desires amidst pleasures, who is devoid of all attachment, fear and anger—that sage is said to be of steady wisdom.

57. He who is free from affection everywhere, and who getting whatever good or evils neither welcomes nor hates them has steady wisdom.

SRIMAD-BHAGAVAD-GITA

यदा संहरते चायं कूर्मोऽङ्गानीव सर्वशः ।
इन्द्रियाणीन्द्रियार्थेभ्य-स्तस्य प्रज्ञा प्रतिष्ठिता ॥ ५८ ॥

विषया विनिवर्तन्ते निराहारस्य देहिनः ।
रसवर्जं रसोऽप्यस्य परं दृष्ट्वा निवर्तते ॥ ५९ ॥

58. And when he completely withdraws his senses from the sense-objects, even as a tortoise its limbs, (then) his wisdom is steady.

59. From an abstemious embodied being (man) sense-objects fall off, but not the relish (for them) ; but even this relish of the man of steady wisdom ceases when that supreme Being is realized.

यततो ह्यपि कौन्तेय पुरुषस्य विपश्चितः ।
इन्द्रियाणि प्रमाथीनि हरन्ति प्रसभं मनः ॥ ६० ॥

तानि सर्वाणि संयम्य युक्त आसीत मत्परः ।
वशे हि यस्येन्द्रियाणि तस्य प्रज्ञा प्रतिष्ठिता ॥ ६१ ॥

60. The turbulent senses, O son of Kunti, forcibly lead astray the mind of even the struggling wise person.

61. Controlling all these (senses), the self-controlled one should sit meditating on Me. Verily, his wisdom is steady, whose senses are under control.

ध्यायतो विषयान् पुंसः सङ्गस्तेषूपजायते ।
सङ्गात् सञ्जायते कामः कामात् क्रोधोऽभिजायते ॥ ६२ ॥

क्रोधाद्भवति संमोहः संमोहात् स्मृतिविभ्रमः ।
स्मृतिभ्रंशाद् बुद्धिनाशो बुद्धिनाशात् प्रणश्यति ॥६३॥

62-63. For a person thinking of the sense-objects there grows an attachment for them; frem attachment arises desire, from desire results anger, from anger results delusion, from delusion results confusion of memory, from confusion of memory results destruction of intelligence and from destruction of ientelligence he perishes.

रागद्वेष-वियुक्तैस्तु विषया-निन्द्रियैश्चरन् ।
आत्मवश्यै-र्विधेयात्मा प्रसाद-मधिगच्छति ॥ ६४ ॥

प्रसादे सर्वदुःखानां हानि-रस्योपजायते ।
प्रसन्न-चेतसो ह्याशु बुद्धिः पर्यवतिष्ठते ॥ ६५ ॥

64. But that person of controlled self who moves about amidst sense-objects with the senses governed by the self and free from attachment and aversion,—he attains serenity.

65. When this serenity is attained there results the destruction of all his misery. Verily, the wisdom of the serene-minded one gets steady soon.

SRIMAD-BHAGAVAD-GITA

नास्ति बुद्धि-रयुक्तस्य न चायुक्तस्य भावना ।
न चाभावयतः शान्ति-रशान्तस्य कुतः सुखम् ॥ ६६ ॥

इन्द्रियाणां हि चरतां यन्मनोऽनुविधीयते ।
तदस्य हरति प्रज्ञां वायु-र्नावमिवांभसि ॥ ६७ ॥

66. For the uncontrolled person there is no knowledge, nor is there meditation for him; and for the unmedi-
tative person there is no peace, and for one bereft of peace
how can there be happiness?

67. Whichever of the wandering senses the mind
follows, that one carries away his wisdom as the wind a ship
on the sea.

THE WAY OF DISCRIMINATION

तस्माद्यस्य महाबाहो निगृहीतानि सर्वशः ।
इन्द्रियाणीन्द्रियार्थेभ्य-स्तस्य प्रज्ञा प्रतिष्ठिता ॥ ६८ ॥

या निशा सर्वभूतानां तस्यां जागर्ति संयमी ।
यस्यां जाग्रति भूतानि सा निशा पश्यतो मुनेः ॥ ६९ ॥

68. Therefore, O mighty-armed one, he whose senses are well controlled from their objects has steady wisdom.

69. That which to all creatures is night, is where the man of self-control is wide awake, and that in which (all) creatures are wide awake is night to the sage who sees.

आपूर्यमाण-मचलप्रतिष्ठं-समुद्रमापः प्रविशन्ति यद्वत् ।
तद्वत्कामा यं प्रविशन्ति सर्वे स शान्ति-मामोति न कामकामी ॥
विहाय कामान् यः सर्वान् पुमांश्चरति निस्पृहः ।
निर्ममो निरहङ्कारः स शान्ति-मधिगच्छति ॥ ७१ ॥

70. He attains peace into whom all sense-objects enter, even as rivers enter an ocean which is unaffected though being ever filled, and not one who is desirous of enjoyments.

71. That person who is giving up all sense-objects goes about unattached, devoid of the idea of ownership and free from egoism—he attains peace.

एषा ब्राह्मी स्थितिः पार्थ नैनां प्राप्य विमुह्यति ।
स्थित्वास्यामन्तकालेऽपि ब्रह्मनिर्वाण-मृच्छति ॥ ७२ ॥

72. This is the Brāhmī state, O Pārtha (Arjuna), attaining it one is not (again) deluded; one who rests in it, even at the time of death, attains Nirvāna in Brahman.

इति श्रीमद्भगवद्गीतासूपनिषत्सु ब्रह्मविद्यायां योगशास्त्रे
श्रीकृष्णार्जुनसंवादे सांख्ययोगो नाम
द्वितीयोऽध्यायः ॥

॥ तृतीयोऽध्यायः ॥

Chapter III

(कर्मयोगः)

THE WAY OF ACTION

अर्जुन उवाच—

ज्यायसी चेत्कर्मणस्ते मता बुद्धि-र्जनार्दन ।
तत्किं कर्मणि घोरे मां नियोजयसि केशव ॥ १ ॥

Arjuna said:

1. If in Your opinion, O Janārdana, knowledge is superior to action, then why do You, O Keśava, engage me in this terrific action?

व्यामिश्रेणेव वाक्येन बुद्धिं मोहयसीव मे ।
तदेकं वद निश्चित्य येन श्रेयोऽहमाप्नुयाम् ॥ २ ॥

श्रीभगवानुवाच—
लोकेऽस्मिन्द्विविधा निष्ठा पुरा प्रोक्ता मयानघ ।
ज्ञानयोगेन साङ्ख्यानां कर्मयोगेन योगिनाम् ॥ ३ ॥

2. By (these) apparently conflicting words You seem to confuse my understanding; tell (me) definitely that one thing by which I can attain final beatitude.

The Blessed Lord said:

3. O sinless one (Arjuna), a twofold faith has been declared by Me earlier for this human race: the way of knowledge for the Sānkhyas, and the way of action for the Yogis.

SRIMAD-BHAGAVAD-GITA

न कर्मणा-मनारम्भा-न्नैष्कर्म्यं पुरुषोऽश्नुते ।
न च संन्यसनादेव सिद्धिं समधिगच्छति ॥ ४ ॥

न हि कश्चित् क्षणमपि जातु तिष्ठत्यकर्मकृत् ।
कार्यते ह्यवशः कर्म सर्वः प्रकृतिजैर्गुणैः ॥ ५ ॥

4. By not doing work a person does not reach inactivity, nor does he attain perfection by mere renunciation (of
action).

5. Verily, no one ever remains inactive even for a
moment; for all are forcibly made to act by the qualities
born of Prakriti.

कर्मेन्द्रियाणि संयम्य य आस्ते मनसा स्मरन् ।
इन्द्रियार्थान्विमूढात्मा मिथ्याचारः स उच्यते ॥ ६ ॥

यस्त्विन्द्रियाणि मनसा नियम्यारभतेऽर्जुन ।
कर्मेन्द्रियैः कर्मयोग-मसक्तः स विशिष्यते ॥ ७ ॥

6. That fool, who (outwardly) controlling the organs, of action keeps dwelling on sense objects with the mind, is called a hypocrite.

7. But he, O Arjuna, who controlling the organs by the mind, performs Karma-Yoga with the organs of action being unattached—he excels.

नियतं कुरु कर्म त्वं कर्म ज्यायो ह्यकर्मणः ।
शरीरयात्राऽपि च ते न प्रसिद्ध्ये-दकर्मणः ॥ ८ ॥

यज्ञार्थात् कर्मणोऽन्यत्र लोकोऽयं कर्मबन्धनः ।
तदर्थं कर्म कौन्तेय मुक्तसङ्गः समाचर ॥ ९ ॥

8. Perform the prescribed duties : for action is superior to inaction ; moreover, if you are inactive, even the maintenance of your body will be impossible.

9. This world is bound by action other than that done for sacrifice ; (therefore) perform actions for the sake of that, O son of Kunti (Arjuna), free from attachment.

सहयज्ञाः प्रजाः सृष्ट्वा पुरोवाच प्रजापतिः ।
अनेन प्रसविष्यध्व-मेष वोऽस्त्विष्टकामधुक् ॥ १० ॥

देवान्भावयतानेन ते देवा भावयन्तु वः ।
परस्परं भावयन्तः श्रेयः परमवाप्स्यथ ॥ ११ ॥

10. Prajāpati, creating of yore beings who co-exist with a sacrifice, said; "By this you multiply, let this yield you covetable objects of desire.

11. "By this entertain the gods and let the gods entertain you; entertaining each other you will both attain supreme good.

SRIMAD-BHAGAVAD-GITA

इष्टान् भोगान्हि वो देवा दास्यन्ते यज्ञ-भाविताः ।
तैर्दत्ता-नप्रदायैभ्यो यो भुङ्क्ते स्तेन एव सः ॥ १२ ॥

यज्ञशिष्टाशिनः सन्तो मुच्यन्ते सर्वकिल्बिषैः ।
भुञ्जते ते त्वघं पापा ये पचन्त्यात्मकारणात् ॥ १३ ॥

12. "Being entertained by sacrifices the gods will surely bestow on you the desired enjoyments. He who enjoys what is given by them without offering it to them, is indeed a thief.

13. "The good who partake of the remnants of a sacrifice are freed from all sins; but those sinful persons who cook for their own sake, partake of sin."

THE WAY OF ACTION

अन्नाद्भवन्ति भूतानि पर्जन्या-दन्नसम्भवः ।
यज्ञाद्भवति पर्जन्यो यज्ञः कर्म-समुद्भवः ॥ १४ ॥

कर्म ब्रह्मोद्भवं विद्धि ब्रह्माक्षरसमुद्भवम् ।
तस्मात् सर्वगतं ब्रह्म नित्यं यज्ञे प्रतिष्ठितम् ॥ १५ ॥

14. Beings are born from food, food is produced from rain, rain comes from a sacrifice, and a sacrifice results from action.

15. Know that action originates from Brahman (the Veda), and Brahman originates from the Imperishable. Therefore the all-pervading Brahman (Veda) eternally rests in the sacrifice.

SRIMAD-BHAGAVAD-GITA

एवं प्रवर्तितं चक्रं नानुवर्तयतीह यः ।
अघायु-रिन्द्रियारामो मोघं पार्थ स जीवति ॥ १६ ॥

यस्त्वात्मरतिरेव स्या-दात्मतृप्तश्च मानवः ।
आत्मन्येव च संतुष्ट-स्तस्य कार्यं न विद्यते ॥ १७॥

16. He who does not follow here this cycle thus set
revolving, who leads a sinful life and delights in the senses,
in vain, O Pārtha (Arjuna), does he live.

17. But that person who delights only in the Self, is
satisfied with the Self, is contented in the Self alone, has no
duties to perform.

नैव तस्य कृतेनार्थो नाकृतेनेह कश्चन ।
न चास्य सर्वभूतेषु कश्चिदर्थव्यपाश्रयः ॥ १८ ॥

तस्मा-दसक्तः सततं कार्यं कर्म समाचर ।
असक्तो ह्याचरन् कर्म परमाप्नोति पूरुषः ॥ १९ ॥

18. He has nothing to gain by action or (lose) by inaction in this world; nor does he depend on any being for attaining his purpose.

19. Therefore always perform action which has to be done, unattached; verily, man attains the highest by performing action unattached.

SRIMAD-BHAGAVAD-GITA

कर्मणैव हि संसिद्धि-मास्थिता जनकादयः ।
लोकसंग्रह-मेवापि संपश्यन् कर्तु-मर्हसि ॥ २० ॥

यद्यदाचरति श्रेष्ठ-स्तत्तदेवेतरो जनः ।
स यत्प्रमाणं कुरुते लोक-स्तदनुवर्तते ॥ २१ ॥

20. By action alone Janaka and others realized perfection. Even considering the incentive to people you should perform action.

21. Whatever a great man does others also copy; that which he accepts as authority, people only follow.

THE WAY OF ACTION

न मे पार्थास्ति कर्तव्यं त्रिषु लोकेषु किञ्चन ।
नानवाप्तम्-अवाप्तव्यं वर्त एव च कर्मणि ॥ २२ ॥

यदि ह्यहं न वर्तेयं जातु कर्मण्यतन्द्रितः ।
मम वर्त्मानुवर्तन्ते मनुष्याः पार्थ सर्वशः ॥ २३ ॥

22. I have no duty to perform, O Pārtha (Arjuna), nor is there anything in the three worlds unattained which is to be attained, still I am engaged in action.

23. If ever I cease to be vigilantly engaged in action, O Pārtha, (then) people (would) follow My footsteps in everyway.

SRIMAD-BHAGAVAD-GITA

उत्सीदेयु-रिमे लोका न कुर्यां कर्म चेदहम् ।
सङ्करस्य च कर्ता स्या-मुपहन्या-मिमाः प्रजाः ॥ २४ ॥
सक्ताः कर्म-ण्यविद्वांसो यथा कुर्वन्ति भारत ।
कुर्या-द्विद्वां-स्तथासक्त-श्चिकीर्षु-र्लोकसंग्रहम् ॥ २५ ॥

24. If I cease doing work, these worlds would be ruined, and I should be causing an admixture of castes and destroying these beings.

25. As the ignorant perform action being attached to it, even so, O descendant of Bharata (Arjuna). should the wise perform action unattached, desiring the welfare of the world.

THE WAY OF ACTION

न बुद्धिभेदं जनयेद्‌अज्ञानां कर्मसङ्गिनाम्‌ ।
जोषयेत्‌ सर्वकर्माणि विद्वान्‌ युक्तः समाचरन्‌ ॥ २६ ॥

प्रकृतेः क्रियमाणानि गुणैः कर्माणि सर्वशः ।
अहङ्कार-विमूढात्मा कर्ताहमिति मन्यते ॥ २७ ॥

26. The wise man should not unsettle the faith of the ignorant who are attached to work. He should make them devoted to all work, performing action himself intently.

27. Actions are done in all cases by the Gunas of Prakriti. He whose mind is deluded through egoism thinks, ' I am the doer.'

SRIMAD-BHAGAVAD-GITA

तत्त्वावित्तु महाबाहो गुण-कर्म-विभागयोः ।
गुणा गुणेषु वर्तन्त इति मत्वा न सज्जते ॥ २८ ॥

प्रकृते गुण-संमूढाः सज्जन्ते गुणकर्मसु ।
तानकृत्स्नविदो मन्दान् कृत्स्नविन्न विचालयेत् ॥२९॥

28. But he who knows, O mighty-armed one, the truth
as to the differentiation of the senses (Gunas) and their
functions (from the Self)—he, knowing that the Gunas or
senses rest in the Gunas or sense-objects, is not attached.

29. Being deluded by the constituents of Prakriti
(Nature), people get attached to the senses and their functions. He who knows everything should not unsettle these
people who are dull-witted and imperfect in knowledge.

मयि सर्वाणि कर्माणि संन्यस्याध्यात्म-चेतसा ।
निराशी-निर्ममो भूत्वा युध्यस्व विगत-ज्वरः ॥३०॥

ये मे मतमिदं नित्य-मनुतिष्ठन्ति मानवाः ।
श्रद्धावन्तोऽनसूयन्तो मुच्यन्ते तेऽपि कर्मभिः ॥३१॥

30. Renouncing all actions in Me, with your mind resting on the Self, and giving up hope and idea of ownership, fight, being free from fever.

31. Those men who ever practise this teaching of Mine with faith and without cavilling, are also freed from actions.

SRIMAD-BHAGAVAD-GITA

येत्वेत-दभ्यसूयन्तो नानुतिष्ठन्ति मे मतम् ।
सर्वज्ञान-विमूढांस्तान्विद्धि नष्टानचेतसः ॥ ३२ ॥

सदृशं चेष्टते स्वस्याः प्रकृते-र्ज्ञानवानपि ।
प्रकृतिं यान्ति भूतानि निग्रहः किं करिष्यति ॥३३॥

32. But those who carp at this teaching of Mine and
do not practise it—know such fools, bereft of all knowledge,
to be doomed.

33. Even a wise man acts according to his own dis-
position ; beings follow (their) nature ; what can restraint
do ?

इन्द्रियस्येन्द्रियस्याथ रागद्वेषौ व्यवस्थितौ ।
तयोर्न वशमागच्छेत्तौ ह्यस्य परिपन्थिनौ ॥ ३४ ॥

श्रेयान् स्वधर्मो विगुणः परधर्मात् स्वनुष्ठितात् ।
स्वधर्मे निधनं श्रेयः परधर्मो भयावहः ॥ ३५ ॥

34. In respect of each of the senses, attachments and aversions to objects are fixed. One should not come under their sway, for they are impediments in one's way.

35. Better is one's own duty, though defective, than another's duty well performed. Death in one's own duty is better; the duty of another is fraught with fear.

अर्जुन उवाच—
अथ केन प्रयुक्तोऽयं पापं चरति पूरुषः ।
अनिच्छन्नपि वार्ष्णेय बलादिव नियोजितः ॥ ३६ ॥

श्रीभगवानुवाच—
काम एष क्रोध एष रजोगुण-समुद्भवः ।
महाशनो महापाप्मा विद्ध्येन-मिह वैरिणम् ॥३७॥

Arjuna said:

36. Prompted by what, does a man commit sin, even though unwilling, O Vārshneya (Sri Krishna), being constrained, as it were, by force ?

The Blessed Lord said:

37. This is desire, this is anger, born of the constituent (of Prakriti called) Rajas—of inordinate appetite and most sinful. Know it to be an enemy here.

धूमेनाव्रियते वह्नि-र्यथादर्शो मलेन च ।
यथोल्बेनावृतो गर्भ-स्तथा तेनेदमावृतम् ॥ ३८ ॥
आवृतं ज्ञान-मेतेन ज्ञानिनो नित्यवैरिणा ।
कामरूपेण कौन्तेय दुष्पूरेणानलेन च ॥ ३९ ॥

38. As fire is enveloped by smoke, as a mirror is covered by dust, as a foetus is enveloped by the amnion, even so is this covered by it.

39. O son of Kunti (Arjuna), knowledge is covered by this eternal enemy of the wise in the form of desire, which is like an insatiable fire.

SRIMAD-BHAGAVAD-GITA

इन्द्रियाणि मनोबुद्धि-रस्याधिष्ठान-मुच्यते ।
एतै-र्विमोहयत्येष ज्ञान-मावृत्य देहिनम् ॥ ४० ॥

तस्माच्च-मिन्द्रिया-ण्यादौ नियम्य भरतर्षभ ।
पाप्मानं प्रजहि ह्येनं ज्ञानविज्ञान-नाशनम् ॥ ४१ ॥

40. The senses, the mind, and the intellect are said to be its seat; covering knowledge by these, it deludes the embodied being.

41. Therefore, controlling the senses at the very outset, O best of the Bharatas (Arjuna), kill this sinful thing which destroys realization and knowledge.

इन्द्रियाणि पराण्याहु-रिन्द्रियेभ्यः परं मनः ।
मनसस्तु परा बुद्धिर्यो बुद्धेः परस्तु सः ॥ ४२ ॥
एवं बुद्धेः परं बुद्ध्वा संस्तभ्यात्मानमात्मना ।
जहि शत्रुं महाबाहो कामरूपं दुरासदम् ॥ ४३ ॥

इति श्रीमद्भगवद्गीतासूपनिषत्सु ब्रह्मविद्यायां योगशास्त्रे
श्रीकृष्णार्जुनसंवादे कर्मयोगो नाम तृतीयोऽध्यायः ॥

42. The senses are said to be superior (to their objects); superior to the senses is the mind; but superior to the mind is the intellect; while that which is superior to the intellect is the Self.

43. Thus knowing that which is beyond the intellect, and controlling the self (mind) by the self (intellect), kill, O mighty-armed one (Arjuna), the enemy in the form of desire, which is difficult to conquer.

|| चतुर्थोऽध्यायः ||

CHAPTER IV

(ज्ञानकर्मसन्न्यासयोगः)

THE WAY OF KNOWLEDGE

श्रीभगवानुवाच—

इमं विवस्वते योगं प्रोक्तवा-नह-मव्ययम् ।
विवस्वान् मनवे प्राह मनुरिक्ष्वाकवे ऽब्रवीत् ॥१॥

The Blessed Lord said:

I. This eternal Yoga I taught to Vivaswat, Vivaswat taught it to Manu and Manu taught it to Ikshvāku.

THE WAY OF KNOWLEDGE

एवं परम्परा-प्राप्त-मिमं राजर्षयो विदुः ।
स कालेनेह महता योगो नष्टः परंतप ॥ २ ॥

स एवायं मया तेऽद्य योगः प्रोक्तः पुरातनः ।
भक्तोऽसि मे सखा चेति रहस्यं ह्येत-दुत्तमम् ॥३॥

2. This (Yoga), thus traditionally handed down, the royal sages knew. Through the great lapse of time this Yoga is lost in this world, O scorcher of foes.

3. That very ancient Yoga has been taught by Me to you this day, since you are my devotee and friend; for this is a supreme secret.

अर्जुन उवाच—

अपरं भवतो जन्म परं जन्म विवस्वतः ।
कथमेत-द्विजानीयां त्वमादौ प्रोक्तवानिति ॥ ४ ॥

श्रीभगवानुवाच—

बहूनि मे व्यतीतानि जन्मानि तव चार्जुन ।
तान्यहं वेद सर्वाणि न त्वं वेत्थ परंतप ॥ ५ ॥

4. Later is Your birth and Vivaswat's birth earlier; how am I to understand this, that You taught this (to him) at the beginning?

The Blessed Lord said:

5. Many lives have I passed through as also yourself; I know them all, but you do not know them, O scorcher of foes.

अजोऽपि सन्नव्ययात्मा भूताना-मीश्वरोऽपि सन् ।
प्रकृतिं स्वामधिष्ठाय संभवा-म्यात्ममायया ॥ ६ ॥

यदा यदा हि धर्मस्य ग्लानि-र्भवति भारत ।
अभ्युत्थान-मधर्मस्य तदात्मानं सृजाम्यहम् ॥७॥

6. Though I am birthless, immutable and the Lord of creatures, yet resorting to My Prakriti, I come into being through My own inscrutable power (Māyā).

7. Whenever, O descendant of Bharata, righteousness declines and unrighteousness prevails, I manifest Myself.

SRIMAD-BHAGAVAD-GITA

परित्राणाय साधूनां विनाशाय च दुष्कृताम् ।
धर्म-संस्थापनार्थाय संभवामि युगे युगे ॥ ८ ॥

जन्म कर्म च मे दिव्यमेवं यो वेत्ति तत्त्वतः ।
त्यक्त्वा देहं पुनर्जन्म नैति मामेति सोऽर्जुन ॥९॥

8. For the protection of the righteous and the destruction of the wicked, and for the establishment of religion, I come into being from age to age.

9. He who thus knows truly My divine birth and work, is no more born after death ; he attains Me, O Arjuna.

वीत-राग-भय-क्रोधा मन्मया मामुपाश्रिताः ।
बहवो ज्ञानतपसा पूता मद्भाव-मागताः ॥ १० ॥

ये यथा मां प्रपद्यन्ते तांस्तथैव भजाम्यहम् ।
मम वर्त्मानुवर्तन्ते मनुष्याः पार्थ सर्वशः ॥ ११ ॥

10. Free from attachment, fear and anger, with their minds intent on Me, purified by knowledge and penance, many have attained My Being.

11. By whatsoever way men worship Me, even so do I accept them; for, in all ways, O Pārtha, men walk in My path.

SRIMAD-BHAGAVAD-GITA

कांक्षन्तः कर्मणां सिद्धिं यजन्त इह देवताः ।
क्षिप्रं हि मानुषे लोके सिद्धि-र्भवति कर्मजा ॥ १२ ॥

चातुर्वर्ण्यं मया सृष्टं गुण-कर्म-विभागशः ।
तस्य कर्तारमपि मां विद्ध्यकर्तार-मव्ययम् ॥ १३ ॥

12. People seeking the fruit of actions worship the gods in this world; for in this world of men the fruit of action comes quickly.

13. The four castes were created by Me according to differences in aptitudes and actions (of men). Though the author of them, know Me the immutable as non-agent.

न मां कर्माणि लिम्पन्ति न मे कर्मफले स्पृहा।
इति मां योऽभिजानाति कर्मभिर्न स बध्यते ॥ १४ ॥

एवं ज्ञात्वा कृतं कर्म पूर्वैरपि मुमुक्षुभिः।
कुरु कर्मैव तस्मात्त्वं पूर्वैः पूर्वतरं कृतम् ॥ १५ ॥

14. Actions do not touch Me, nor have I any desire for their fruit—he who knows Me thus, is not bound by actions.

15. Thus knowing, even the ancient seekers of Liberation performed work of yore. Therefore perform work alone done by the ancients.

SRIMAD-BHAGAVAD-GITA

किं कर्म किमकर्मेति कवयोऽप्यत्र मोहिताः ।
तत्ते कर्म प्रवक्ष्यामि यज्ज्ञात्वा मोक्ष्यसेऽशुभात् ॥ १६ ॥

कर्मणो ह्यपि बोद्धव्यं बोद्धव्यं च विकर्मणः ।
अकर्मणश्च बोद्धव्यं गहना कर्मणो गतिः ॥ १७ ॥

16. Even the wise are deluded as to what is action and what is inaction. I shall expound to you that action knowing which you will be free from all ills.

17. There is (something) to know about prescribed action and about action that is prohibited, as also about inaction; the way of action is mysterious.

THE WAY OF KNOWLEDGE

कर्मण्यकर्म यः पश्ये-दकर्मणि च कर्म यः ।
स बुद्धिमान् मनुष्येषु स युक्तः कृत्स्नकर्मकृत् ॥१८॥

यस्य सर्वे समारम्भाः कामसङ्कल्प-वर्जिताः ।
ज्ञानाग्नि-दग्धकर्माणं तमाहुः पण्डितं बुधाः ॥१९॥

18. He who sees inaction in action and action in inaction is wise amongst men : he is poised and a performer of all actions.

19. He whose actions are all free from the hankering for desires, whose actions have been burnt by the fire of knowledge, him the wise call a sage.

SRIMAD-BHAGAVAD-GITA

त्यक्त्वा कर्मफलासङ्गं नित्यतृप्तो निराश्रयः ।
कर्मण्यभि-प्रवृत्तोऽपि नैव किञ्चित् करोति सः ॥२०॥

निराशी-र्यतचित्तात्मा त्यक्त-सर्व-परिग्रहः ।
शारीरं केवलं कर्म कुर्व-न्नाप्नोति किल्बिषम् ॥२१॥

20. Renouncing the attachment for action and its fruit, ever contented, and without any refuge, he does not do anything, even though engaged in action.

21. Bereft of desire, controlled in mind and body, with all possessions relinquished and doing merely bodily action, he does not get tainted.

यदृच्छा-लाभ-संतुष्टो द्वन्द्वातीतो विमत्सरः ।
समः सिद्धावसिद्धौ च कृत्वापि न निबध्यते ॥२२॥
गतसङ्गस्य मुक्तस्य ज्ञानावस्थित-चेतसः ।
यज्ञायाचरतः कर्म समग्रं प्रविलीयते ॥ २३ ॥

22. Contented with what chance brings, transcending the pair of opposites, free from jealousy, and unperturbed in success and failure, he is not bound even though performing actions.

23. He who is devoid of attachment, free, whose mind is established in knowledge, and who does work as a sacrifice (for the Lord)—his entire action melts away.

SRIMAD-BHAGAVAD-GITA

ब्रह्मार्पणं ब्रह्म हविर्ब्रह्माग्नौ ब्रह्मणा हुतम् ।
ब्रह्मैव तेन गन्तव्यं ब्रह्मकर्म-समाधिना ॥ २४ ॥
दैवमेवापरे यज्ञं योगिनः पर्युपासते ।
ब्रह्माग्नावपरे यज्ञं यज्ञेनैवोपजुह्वति ॥ २५ ॥

24. The ladle is Brahman, the oblation is Brahman, it is offered by Brahman in the fire, which is Brahman, Brahman alone he attains who sees Brahman in action.

25. Sacrifices to the gods alone other (Karma-Yogins) resort to. (Still) others offer the sacrifice by way of a sacrifice in the fire of Brahman alone.

श्रोत्रादीनीन्द्रियाण्यन्ये संयमाग्निषु जुह्वति ।
शब्दादीन्विषयानन्य इन्द्रियाग्निषु जुह्वति ॥२६॥

सर्वाणीन्द्रिय-कर्माणि प्राणकर्माणि चापरे ।
आत्मसंयमयोगाग्नौ जुह्वति ज्ञानदीपिते ॥ २७ ॥

26. Others offer the ear and other senses as sacrifice in the fire of self-control; others, again, offer sound and other objects of the senses in the fires of the senses.

27. Others offer the functions of all the organs and Prāṇas in the fire of the Yoga of self-control lighted by knowledge.

8

SRIMAD-BHAGAVAD-GITA

द्रव्ययज्ञा-स्तपोयज्ञा योगयज्ञा-स्तथापरे ।
स्वाध्याय-ज्ञानयज्ञाश्च यतयः संशितव्रताः ॥२८॥

अपाने जुह्वति प्राणं प्राणेऽपानं तथापरे ।
प्राणापानगती रुद्ध्वा प्राणायाम-परायणाः ॥२९॥

28. There are others who sacrifice through gifts, others (again) who sacrifice through penance, and still others who sacrifice through Yoga ; while there are others, aspirants of austere vows, who sacrifice through knowledge from scriptural studies.

29. (Still) others, devoted to the control of the vital force (Prāṇāyāma), offer as a sacrifice the outgoing breath (Prāṇa) in the incoming (Apāna), as also the incoming breath in the outgoing, after restraining the activity of the incoming and the outgoing breath.

अपरे नियताहाराः प्राणान् प्राणेषु जुह्वति ।
सर्वेऽप्येते यज्ञविदो यज्ञक्षपित-कल्मषाः ॥ ३० ॥
यज्ञशिष्टामृतभुजो यान्ति ब्रह्म सनातनम् ।
नायं लोकोऽस्त्ययज्ञस्य कुतोऽन्यः कुरुसत्तम ॥ ३१ ॥

30. Others again, who regulate their food, offer as a sacrifice the functions of the senses in the senses. All these indeed are knowers of the sacrifices, purified of their sins through sacrifices.

31. Eating of the ambrosial food after the sacrifice, they attain the eternal Brahman. (Even) this world is not for the non-sacrificing, much less the other, O best of the Kurus (Arjuna).

एवं बहुविधा यज्ञा वितता ब्रह्मणो मुखे ।
कर्मजान्विद्धि तान् सर्वानेवं ज्ञात्वा विमोक्ष्यसे॥३२॥
श्रेयान् द्रव्यमयाद्यज्ञा-ज्ज्ञानयज्ञः परंतप ।
सर्वं कर्माखिलं पार्थ ज्ञाने परिसमाप्यते ॥ ३३ ॥

32. Thus various sacrifices are prescribed by the Vedas. Know all these to be born of action : knowing thus you will be free.

33. The sacrifice through knowledge is superior to sacrifice performed with materials, O scorcher of foes ; all actions in their entirety, O Pārtha, are comprised in knowledge.

तद्विद्धि प्रणिपातेन परिप्रश्नेन सेवया ।
उपदेक्ष्यन्ति ते ज्ञानं ज्ञानिन-स्तत्त्वदर्शिनः ॥ ३४ ॥
यज्ज्ञात्वा न पुन-र्मोह-मेवं यास्यसि पाण्डव ।
येन भूतान्यशेषेण द्रक्ष्य-स्यात्मन्यथो मयि ॥ ३५ ॥

34. Acquire that through prostration, inquiry and service. The wise who are knowers of the Truth will instruct you in wisdom.

35. Acquiring which, O son of Pāndu, you will no more be thus deluded; by which you will see all creatures in yourself and then in Me.

SRIMAD-BHAGAVAD-GITA

अपि चेदसि पापेभ्यः सर्वेभ्यः पापकृत्तमः ।
सर्वं ज्ञान-प्लवेनैव वृजिनं संतरिष्यसि ॥ ३६ ॥

यथैधांसि समिद्धोऽग्नि-र्भस्मसात् कुरुतेऽर्जुन ।
ज्ञानाग्निः सर्वकर्माणि भस्मसात् कुरुते तथा ॥३७॥

36. Eveu if you be the worst sinner amongst all sinners, (yet) you will cross all sin by the boat of knowledge alone.

37. Even as a blazing fire burns the fuel to ashes, O Arjuna, even so the fire of knowledge burns to ashes all actions.

न हि ज्ञानेन सदृशं पवित्र-मिह विद्यते ।
तत्स्वयं योग-संसिद्धः कालेनात्मनि विन्दति ॥३८॥

श्रद्धावाँ-ल्लभते ज्ञानं तत्परः संयतेन्द्रियः ।
ज्ञानं लब्ध्वा परां शान्ति-मचिरेणाधिगच्छति ॥३९॥

38. There is indeed nothing so purifying here as knowledge. One perfected in Yoga attains that automatically in himself in time.

39. The man of faith, zeal, and self-control attains knowledge: having attained knowledge, he immediately attains supreme Peace.

SRIMAD-BHAGAVAD-GITA

अज्ञश्चाश्रद्दधानश्च संशयात्मा विनश्यति ।
नायं लोकोऽस्ति न परो न सुखं संशयात्मनः॥४०॥

योगसंन्यस्त-कर्माणं ज्ञानसंछिन्न-संशयम् ।
आत्मवन्तं न कर्माणि निबध्नन्ति धनञ्जय ॥४१॥

40. He who is ignorant, wanting in faith, and of a doubting mind is ruined; for the doubting man there is neither this nor the other world, nor happiness.

41. (But) he who has renounced (the fruit of) actions through Yoga, whose doubts have been destroyed by knowledge, and who is self-possessed, O Dhananjaya (Arjuna), is not bound by actions.

तस्मा-दज्ञान-संभूतं हृत्स्थं ज्ञानासिनात्मनः ।
छित्त्वैनं संशयं योग-मातिष्ठोत्तिष्ठ भारत ॥ ४२ ॥

इति श्रीमद्भगवद्गीतासूपनिषत्सु ब्रह्मविद्यायां योगशास्त्रे
श्रीकृष्णार्जुनसंवादे ज्ञानकर्मसन्न्यासयोगो नाम
चतुर्थोऽध्यायः ॥

42. Therefore, O descendant of Bharata, destroying this doubt born of ignorance of the Self and seated in the heart, with the sword of knowledge, take to Yoga and arise.

॥ पञ्चमोऽध्यायः ॥
(सन्न्यासयोगः)

अर्जुन उवाच—

सन्न्यासं कर्मणां कृष्ण पुनर्योगं च शंससि ।
यच्छ्रेय एतयो-रेकं तन्मे ब्रूहि सुनिश्चितम् ॥ १ ॥

Chapter V
RENUNCIATION OF ACTION

Arjuna said:

1. O Krishna, You teach renunciation of actions and again action; tell (me) decisively that one of the two which is good for me.

श्रीभगवानुवाच—
सन्न्यासः कर्मयोगश्च निःश्रेयसकरा-वुभौ ।
तयोस्तु कर्मसन्न्यासात् कर्मयोगो विशिष्यते ॥२॥
ज्ञेयः स नित्य-सन्न्यासी यो न द्वेष्टि न काङ्क्षति ।
निर्द्वन्द्वो हि महाबाहो सुखं बन्धात् प्रमुच्यते ॥३॥

The Blessed Lord said:

2. Renunciation and the performance of (selfless) action both lead to Liberation; but of the two the performance of (selfless) action is superior to the renunciation of action.

3. He who neither dislikes nor desires should be known as a perpetual renouncer of action; for, O mighty-armed one, one who is free from the dual throng is easily freed from bondage.

SRIMAD-BHAGAVAD-GITA

साङ्ख्ययोगौ पृथग्बालाः प्रवदन्ति न पण्डिताः ।
एकम-प्यास्थितः सम्य-गुभयो-र्विन्दते फलम् ॥४॥

यत्साङ्ख्यैः प्राप्यते स्थानं तद्योगैरपि गम्यते ।
एकं साङ्ख्यं च योगं च यः पश्यति स पश्यति ॥५॥

4. The ignorant say that knowledge and (selfless) action are different, (but) not the wise ; practising thoroughly even one, a person attains to the fruit of both.

5. That status which is attained by men of knowledge is also attained by men of (selfless) action ; he sees (truly) who sees the way of knowledge and that of (selfless) action as one.

सन्न्यासस्तु महाबाहो दुःखमाप्तु-मयोगतः ।
योगयुक्तो मुनिर्ब्रह्म नचिरेणाधिगच्छति ॥ ६ ॥
योगयुक्तो विशुद्धात्मा विजितात्मा जितेन्द्रियः ।
सर्वभूतात्मभूतात्मा कुर्वन्नपि न लिप्यते ॥ ७ ॥

6. But renunciation of action, O mighty-armed one, is difficult to attain without performance of (selfless) action; the sage devoted to (selfless) action attains Brahman quickly.

7. He who is devoted to (selfless) action (Yoga) and pure in mind, whose body and senses are under control, and whose Self has become the Self of all, is not touched even though he may be performing work.

नैव किञ्चित् करोमीति युक्तो मन्येत तत्त्ववित् ।
पश्यञ्शृण्वन् स्पृशञ्जिघ्र-न्नश्नन्गच्छन् स्वपञ्श्वसन् ॥८॥

प्रलपन्विसृजन् गृह्ऩन्नुन्मिष-न्निमिषन्नपि ।
इन्द्रियाणीन्द्रियार्थेषु वर्तन्त इति धारयन् ॥ ९ ॥

8-9. The man of selfless action, who knows the Truth, thinks, 'I am not doing anything,' even while seeing, hearing, touching, smelling, eating, going, sleeping, breathing, speaking, excreting, grasping, and opening and closing of the eyelids, believing that the senses rest in the sense-objects.

ब्रह्मण्याधाय कर्माणि सङ्गं त्यक्त्वा करोति यः ।
लिप्यते न स पापेन पद्मपत्र-मिवाम्भसा ॥ १० ॥

कायेन मनसा बुद्ध्या केवलै-रिन्द्रियैरपि ।
योगिनः कर्म कुर्वन्ति सङ्गं त्यक्त्वात्मशुद्धये ॥११॥

10. He who performs actions dedicating them to the Lord and giving up attachment, is not touched by sin, as a lotus leaf by water.

11. Men of selfless action, giving up attachment, perform action through the body, mind, intellect as also the mere senses, for the purification of the mind.

SRIMAD-BHAGAVAD-GITA

युक्तः कर्मफलं त्यक्त्वा शान्ति-मामोति नैष्ठिकीम् ।
अयुक्तः कामकारेण फले सक्तो निबध्यतें ॥ १२ ॥

सर्वकर्माणि मनसा सन्न्यस्यास्ते सुखं वशी ।
नवद्वारे पुरे देही नैव कुर्वन्न कारयन् ॥ १३ ॥

12. The harmonised one, giving up the fruit of action, attains the highest peace ; the non-harmonised one, working under the sway of desire, is attached to the fruit and gets bound.

13. The self-controlled embodied being, renouncing all actions through his mind, rest at ease in the city of nine gates (the body), neither acting nor causing to act.

न कर्तृत्वं न कर्माणि लोकस्य सृजति प्रभुः ।
न कर्मफल-संयोगं स्वभावस्तु प्रवर्तते ॥ १४ ॥

नादत्ते कस्यचित् पापं न चैव सुकृतं विभुः ।
अज्ञानेनावृतं ज्ञानं तेन मुह्यन्ति जन्तवः ॥ १५ ॥

14. The Lord creates for this world neither agency nor actions nor the union with the fruit of actions; but nature acts.

15. The omnipresent Lord does not accept the sin or virtue of anybody. Knowledge is enveloped by ignorance; because of this beings get deluded.

SRIMAD-BHAGAVAD-GITA

ज्ञानेन तु तद्ज्ञानं येषां नाशित-मात्मनः ।
तेषा-मादित्यव-ज्ज्ञानं प्रकाशयति तत्परम् ॥१६॥

तद्बुद्ध्य-स्तदात्मान-स्तन्निष्ठा-स्तत्परायणाः ।
गच्छन्त्यपुन-रावृत्तिं ज्ञाननिर्धूत-कल्मषाः ॥ १७ ॥

16. But those whose ignorance has been destroyed by the knowledge of the Self—their knowledge, like the sun, manifests that highest Being.

17. Those who are decided on That, whose mind is set in That, who are devoted to That, and whose last resort is That, attain to non-return, with their sins winnowed off by knowledge.

विद्या-विनय-संपन्ने ब्राह्मणे गवि हस्तिनि ।
शुनि चैव श्वपाके च पण्डिताः समदर्शिनः ॥ १८ ॥

इहैव तैर्जितः सर्गो येषां साम्ये स्थितं मनः ।
निर्दोषं हि समं ब्रह्म तस्माद्ब्रह्मणि ते स्थिताः ॥१९॥

18. The wise look with equal eye on a Brāhmana endowed with learning and humility, a cow, an elephant, a dog and an outcaste.

19. Even here is the relative existence conquered by them whose mind rests in equality; for Brahman is even and faultless, therefore are they established in Brahman.

SRIMAD-BHAGAVAD-GITA

न प्रहृष्येत्प्रियं प्राप्य नोद्विजेत् प्राप्य चाप्रियम् ।
स्थिरबुद्धि-रसंमूढो ब्रह्मविद्ब्रह्मणि स्थितः ॥ २० ॥

बाह्य-स्पर्शेष्वसक्तात्मा विन्दत्यात्मनि यत्सुखम् ।
स ब्रह्मयोग युक्तात्मा सुखमक्षय्य-मश्नुते ॥ २१ ॥

20. The knower of Brahman who is established in Brahman; poised in mind and undeluded, is not elated on getting what is pleasant nor feels worried on getting what is unpleasant.

21. He whose mind is unattached to the external objects of the senses attains to the bliss that is in the self; he with his mind identified with Brahman through absorption in It, enjoys undecaying bliss.

ये हि संस्पर्शजा भोगा दुःखयोनय एव ते ।
आद्यन्तवन्तः कौन्तेय न तेषु रमते बुधः ॥ २२ ॥

शक्नोतीहैव यः सोढुं प्राक्शरीर-विमोक्षणात् ।
कामक्रोधोद्भवं वेगं स युक्तः स सुखी नरः ॥ २३ ॥

22. Enjoyments born of sense-objects are indeed the sources of misery: they have, O son of Kunti, a beginning and an end ; the wise man does not joice in them.

23. He who is able to withstand the urge arising from passion and anger in this very life, before the fall of the body, is a poised and happy man.

SRIMAD-BHAGAVAD-GITA

योऽन्तःसुखोऽन्तरारामस्तथान्त-ज्योतिरेव यः ।
स योगी ब्रह्मनिर्वाणं ब्रह्मभूतोऽधिगच्छति ॥ २४

लभन्ते ब्रह्मनिर्वाणं-मृषयः क्षीण-कल्मषाः ।
छिन्नद्वैधा यतात्मानः सर्वभूतहिते रताः ॥ २५ ॥

24. He whose happiness is within, whose rejoicing is within and whose light is within, that Yogi, established in Brahman, attains mergence in Brahman.

25. Sages whose sins have waned away, whose doubts have been dispelled, who have controlled their mind, and who are devoted to the welfare of all beings, attain absorption in Brahman.

कामक्रोध-वियुक्तानां यतीनां यतचेतसाम् ।
अभितो ब्रह्मनिर्वाणं वर्तते विदितात्मनाम् ॥ २६ ॥

स्पर्शान् कृत्वा बहिर्बाह्यां श्चक्षुश्चैवान्तरे भ्रुवोः ।
प्राणापानौ समौ कृत्वा नासाभ्यन्तर-चारिणौ ॥२७॥

26. Sages who are free from passion and anger, who have controlled their mind, and who have realized the Self, attain absorption in Brahman here and hereafter.

27-28. Shutting out external sense-objects, fixing the gaze between the eyebrows, controlling the outgoing and in-

SRIMAD-BHAGAVAD-GITA

यतेन्द्रिय-मनो-बुद्धि-र्मुनि-र्मोक्षपरायणः ।
विगतेच्छा-भय-क्रोधो यः सदा मुक्त एव सः ॥ २८ ॥

coming breaths that move through the nostrils, with the senses, mind and intellect restrained, and free from desire, fear and anger, the sage who has Liberation as his highest goal is indeed ever free.

भोक्तारं यज्ञ-तपसां सर्वलोक-महेश्वरम् ।
सुहृदं सर्वभूतानां ज्ञात्वा मां शान्ति-मृच्छति ॥ २९ ॥

इति श्रीमद्भगवद्गीतासूपनिषत्सु ब्रह्मविद्यायां योगशास्त्रे
श्रीकृष्णार्जुनसंवादे सन्न्यासयोगो नाम
पञ्चमोऽध्यायः ॥

29. Knowing Me, the enjoyer of all sacrifices and asceticism, the great Lord of all the worlds and the well-Wisher of all beings, one attains peace.

॥ षष्ठोऽध्यायः ॥

(ध्यानयोगः)

श्रीभगवानुवाच—

अनाश्रितः कर्मफलं कार्यं कर्म करोति यः ।
स सन्न्यासी च योगी च न निरग्निर्न चाक्रियः ॥१॥

Chapter VI

THE WAY OF CONTEMPLATION

The Blessed Lord said :

1. He who does the prescribed work without caring for its fruit, is a Sannyāsi as also a Yogi, and not he who is without the (sacred) fire and without action.

यं सन्न्यास-मिति प्राहु-र्योगं तं विद्धि पाण्डव ।
न ह्यसन्न्यस्त-सङ्कल्पो योगी भवति कश्चन ॥ २ ॥
आरुरुक्षो-र्मुने-र्योगं कर्म कारण-मुच्यते ।
योगारूढस्य तस्यैव शमः कारण-मुच्यते ॥ ३ ॥

2. Know that which is extolled as Sannyāsa, to be Yoga, O Pāndava (Arjuna). Verily, no one becomes a Yogi without renouncing desire for the fruit of action.

3. For the sage who desires to attain to Yoga, action is said to be the means; and for him alone, when he has attained to Yoga, inaction is said to be the means.

SRIMAD-BHAGAVAD-GITA

यदा हि नेन्द्रियार्थेषु न कर्म-स्वनुषज्जते ।
सर्व-सङ्कल्प-सन्न्यासी योगारूढ-स्तदोच्यते ॥ ४ ॥

उद्धरे-दात्मनात्मानं नात्मान-मवसादयेत् ।
आत्मैव ह्यात्मनो बन्धु-रात्मैव रिपु-रात्मनः ॥ ५ ॥

4. When one habitually renounces all desires and is no more attached either to sense-objects or to actions, then one is said to have attained to Yoga.

5. One should raise oneself through the self, and never lower oneself; for the self alone is one's friend and the self alone is one's enemy.

THE WAY OF CONTEMPLATION

बन्धुरात्मात्मन-स्तस्य येनात्मैवात्मना जितः ।
अनात्मनस्तु शत्रुत्वे वर्तेतात्मैव शत्रुवत् ॥ ६ ॥
जितात्मनः प्रशान्तस्य परमात्मा समाहितः ।
शीतोष्ण-सुखदुःखेषु तथा मानापमानयोः ॥ ७ ॥

6. To him who has conquered the self (body and senses) by his self, the self is his friend; for the uncontrolled man, however, the self alone is adverse like an enemy.

7. The self of one who is self-controlled and serene is alone poised in heat and cold, happiness and misery, as also in honour and dishonour.

SRIMAD-BHAGAVAD-GITA

ज्ञान-विज्ञान-तृप्तात्मा कूटस्थो विजितेन्द्रियः ।
युक्त इत्युच्यते योगी सम-लोष्टाश्म-काञ्चनः ॥८॥

सुहृन्मित्रा-र्युदासीन-मध्यस्थ-द्वेष्य-बन्धुषु ।
साधुष्वपि च पापेषु समबुद्धि-र्विशिष्यते ॥ ९ ॥

8. The Yogi whose self is satisfied through knowledge and realization, who is steady and has the senses under control, and to whom a clod of earth, a stone and gold are of equal value, is said to be steadfast.

9. He excels, who looks equally on a well-wisher, a friend, an enemy, a neutral, an arbiter, a hateful person, a relative and also on the good and the sinful.

योगी युञ्जीत सतत-मात्मानं रहसि स्थितः।
एकाकी यतचित्तात्मा निराशी-रपरिग्रहः ॥ १० ॥

शुचौ देशे प्रतिष्ठाप्य स्थिर-मासन-मात्मनः ।
नात्युच्छ्रितं नातिनीचं चैलाजिन-कुशोत्तरम् ॥११॥

10. The Yogi, with his mind and self (body) subjugated, free from desire, destitute and living alone in solitudes should constantly concentrate his mind.

11-12. In a clean spot fixing his seat firm, neither too high nor too low, made of the Kusha grass, skin and cloth one on top of the other—sitting on that, with the activities of the mind and the senses controlled, concentrating his

SRIMAD-BHAGAVAD-GITA

तत्रैकाग्रं मनः कृत्वा यत-चित्तेन्द्रिय-क्रियः ।
उपविश्यासने युञ्ज्या-द्योग-मात्म-विशुद्धये ॥१२॥

समं काय-शिरो-ग्रीवं धारय-न्नचलं स्थिरः ।
संप्रेक्ष्य नासिकाग्रं स्वं दिश्श्चानवलोकयन् ॥१३॥

प्रशान्तात्मा विगतभी-र्ब्रह्मचारि-व्रते स्थितः ।
मनः संयम्य मच्चित्तो युक्त आसीत मत्परः ॥१४॥

mind, he should practise Yoga for the purification of the
mind.

13-14. Holding the trunk, head and neck erect and
steady, becoming firm, fixing the gaze on the tip of his nose

युञ्जन्नेवं सदात्मानं योगी नियत-मानसः ।
शान्तिं निर्वाण-परमां मत्संस्थामधिगच्छति ॥१५॥
नात्यश्नतस्तु योगोऽस्ति न चैकान्त-मनश्नतः ।
न चाति-स्वप्न-शीलस्य जाग्रतो नैव चार्जुन ॥१६॥

and not looking around, tranquil in mind, fearless, practising continence, controlling the mind, intent on Me, he should sit absorbed having Me as the supreme goal.

15. Thus constantly concentrating the mind, the Yogi, with his mind controlled, attains the peace culminating in final Beatitude in the form of abiding in Me.

16. Yoga is not attained by one who eats too much or who eats nothing at all, nor by him who sleeps too much or who keeps awake (too much), O Arjuna.

SRIMAD-BHAGAVAD-GITA

युक्ताहार-विहारस्य युक्त-चेष्टस्य कर्मसु ।
युक्त-स्वप्नावबोधस्य योगो भवति दुःखहा ॥१७॥

यदा विनियतं चित्त-मात्मन्येवावतिष्ठते ।
निःस्पृहः सर्वकामेभ्यो युक्त इत्युच्यते तदा ॥१८॥

17. He who is moderate in food and movements, in his engagement in actions, and in sleep and wakefulness, attains to Yoga which destroys misery.

18. When the mind, well-controlled, remains fixed in the Self alone, and one is free from craving for all enjoyments, then one is said to have attained Yoga.

यथा दीपो निवातस्थो नेङ्गते सोपमा स्मृता ।
योगिनो यत-चित्तस्य युञ्जतो योग-मात्मनः ॥१९॥

यत्रोपरमते चित्तं निरुद्धं योग-सेवया ।
यत्र चैवात्मनात्मानं पश्यन्नात्मनि तुष्यति ॥२०॥

सुख-मात्यन्तिकं यत्तद्-बुद्धि-ग्राह्य-मतीन्द्रियम् ।
वेत्ति यत्र न चैवायं स्थित-श्चलति तत्त्वतः ॥ २१ ॥

19. Even as a lamp placed in a place free from any breeze does not flicker—this is the simile for a Yogi of controlled mind, practising concentration on the Self.

20-23. That state in which the mind controlled by h practice of concentration gets settled; in which seeing tth

SRIMAD-BHAGAVAD-GITA

यं लब्ध्वा चापरं लाभं मन्यते नाधिकं ततः ।
यस्मिन्स्थितो न दुःखेन गुरुणापि विचाल्यते ॥२२॥

तं विद्याद्-दुःख-संयोगवियोगं योग-संज्ञितम् ।
स निश्चयेन योक्तव्यो योगोऽनिर्विण्ण-चेतसा ॥२३॥ ।

Self by the (purified) mind one is satisfied with the Self; in which one realizes same absolute, transcendent bliss which is experienced through the intellect; established in which one does not waver from the Truth; attaining which one thinks of no other acquisition as greater than that; and established in which, one is not perturbed even by great pain—that, one should know, is designated as Yoga, untouched by all contact with pain. That Yoga should be practised with conviction and without depression of spirits.

सङ्कल्प-प्रभवान् कामांस्त्यक्त्वा सर्वानशेषतः ।
मनसैवेन्द्रिय-ग्रामं विनियम्य समन्ततः ॥ २४ ॥

शनैः शनै-रुपरमेद्-बुद्ध्या धृति-गृहीतया ।
आत्म-संस्थं मनः कृत्वा न किञ्चिदपि चिन्तयेत् ॥२५॥

24. Having completely renounced all desires born of fancy, controlling well the senses from all sides by the mind alone, (Yoga should be practised).

25. One should withdraw by degrees, establishing the mind in the Self by the intellect regulated by concentration, and should not think of anything else.

SRIMAD-BHAGAVAD-GITA

यतो यतो निश्चरति मन-श्चञ्चल-मस्थिरम् ।
ततस्ततो नियम्यैत-दात्मन्येव वशं नयेत् ॥ २६ ॥

प्रशान्त-मनसं ह्येनं योगिनं सुखमुत्तमम् ।
उपैति शान्त-रजसं ब्रह्मभूत-मकल्मषम् ॥ २७ ॥

26. Wheresoever the restless and unsteady mind wanders, from that very object it should be restrained and brought under the control of the Self alone.

27. To this Yogin whose activity (Rajas) has subsided, who is of a tranquil mind, sinless and identified with Brahman, comes supreme bliss.

युञ्जन्नेवं सदात्मानं योगी विगत-कल्मषः ।
सुखेन ब्रह्मसंस्पर्श-मत्यन्तं सुख-मश्नुते ॥ २८ ॥

सर्वभूतस्थ-मात्मानं सर्वभूतानि चात्मनि ।
ईक्षते योग-युक्तात्मा सर्वत्र समदर्शनः ॥ २९ ॥

28. The Yogi entirely free from taint, constantly controlling the mind thus, attains easily the infinite bliss of union with Brahman.

29. The man whose mind is absorbed through Yoga and who sees the same (Brahman) everywhere, sees the Self in all beings and all beings in the Self.

SRIMAD-BHAGAVAD-GITA

यो मां पश्यति सर्वत्र सर्वं च मयि पश्यति ।
तस्याहं न प्रणश्यामि स च मे न प्रणश्यति ॥३०॥

सर्वभूतस्थितं यो मां भजत्येकत्व-मास्थितः ।
सर्वथा वर्तमानोऽपि स योगी मयि वर्तते ॥ ३१ ॥

30.   He who sees Me everywhere and sees all things in
Me, does not lose sight of Me, nor do I of him.

31.   He who worships Me residing in all beings in a
spirit of unity, becomes a Yogi and, whatever his mode of
life, lives in Me.

आत्मौपम्येन सर्वत्र समं पश्यति योऽर्जुन ।
सुखं वा यदि वा दुःखं स योगी परमो मतः ॥३२॥

अर्जुन उवाच—
योऽयं योग-स्त्वया प्रोक्तः साम्येन मधुसूदन ।
एतस्याहं न पश्यामि चञ्चलत्वात् स्थितिं स्थिराम् ॥३३॥

32. He who by comparison with himself looks upon the pleasure and pain in all creatures as similar—that Yogi, O Arjuna, is considered the best.

Arjuna said:
33. For this Yoga that you have described as equanimity, O slayer of Madhu (Sri Krishna), I do not see any permanence, owing to restlessness (of the mind).

चञ्चलं हि मनः कृष्ण प्रमाथि बलवद् दृढम् ।
तस्याहं निग्रहं मन्ये वायोरिव सुदुष्करम् ॥ ३४ ॥

श्री भगवानुवाच—
असंशयं महाबाहो मनो दुर्निग्रहं चलम् ।
अभ्यासेन तु कौन्तेय वैराग्येण च गृह्यते ॥३५॥

34. For the mind, O Krishna, is restless, turbulent, strong and obstinate; I think it is extremely difficult to control like the wind.

The Blessed Lord said:

35. Undoubtedly, O mighty-armed one (Arjuna), the mind is restless and hard to control; yet by practice and dispassion, O son of Kunti, it is controlled.

असंयतात्मना योगो दुष्प्राप इति मे मतिः ।
वश्यात्मना तु यतता शक्यो ऽवाप्तु-मुपायतः ॥३६॥

अर्जुन उवाच—
अयतिः श्रद्धयोपेतो योगा-च्चलित-मानसः ।
अप्राप्य योग-संसिद्धिं कां गतिं कृष्ण गच्छति॥ ३७॥

36. For one whose mind is not controlled, I consider Yoga is hard to attain; but it is attainable by one whose mind is under control and who strives through (the prescribed) means.

Arjuna asked:
37. He who, though endowed with faith, strives not, and whose mind wanders from Yoga—failing to attain the fruition of Yoga, what goal, O Krishna, does a person attain?

SRIMAD-BHAGAVAD-GITA

कच्चिन्नोभय-विभ्रष्ट-श्छिन्नाभ्रमिव नश्यति ।
अप्रतिष्ठो महाबाहो विमूढो ब्रह्मणः पथि ॥ ३८ ॥

एतन्मे संशयं कृष्ण छेत्तु-महस्यशेषतः ।
त्वदन्यः संशयस्यास्य छेत्ता न ह्युपपद्यते ॥ ३९ ॥

38. Does he not, O mighty-armed one, fallen from both and without any support perish like detached cloud, being deluded in the path of Brahman?

39. This doubt of mine, O Krishna, You should dispel in its entirety, for there is none else but You who can remove this doubt.

श्री भगवानुवाच—
पार्थ नैवेह नामुत्र विनाश-स्तस्य विद्यते ।
न हि कल्याणकृत् कश्चिद्-दुर्गतिं तात गच्छति ॥४०॥

प्राप्य पुण्यकृतां लोका-नुषित्वा शाश्वतीः समाः ।
शुचीनां श्रीमतां गेहे योगभ्रष्टोऽभिजायते ॥ ४१ ॥

The Blessed Lord said:

40. Verily neither here nor hereafter, O Pārtha, is there destruction for him: for the doer of good, my child, never comes by evil.

41. Having attained the worlds of the righteous and lived there for many, many years, one who has fallen from Yoga is born again in the house of the pure and prosperous.

SRIMAD-BHAGAVAD-GITA

अथवा योगिनामेव कुले भवति धीमताम् ।
एतद्धि दुर्लभतरं लोके जन्म यदीदृशम् ॥ ४२ ॥

तत्र तं बुद्धि-संयोगं लभते पौर्व-देहिकम् ।
यतते च ततो भूयः संसिद्धौ कुरुनन्दन ॥ ४३ ॥

42. Or he is reborn even in the family of Yogis who are wise ; such a birth is rare indeed in this world.

43. There he comes in contact with knowledge acquired in the previous birth, and strives harder than before for perfection, O descendent of Kuru (Arjuna).

THE WAY OF CONTEMPLATION

पूर्वाभ्यासेन तेनैव ह्रियते ह्यवशोऽपि सः ।
जिज्ञासुरपि योगस्य शब्दब्रह्मातिवर्तते ॥ ४४ ॥

प्रयत्नाद्यतमानस्तु योगी संशुद्ध-किल्बिषः ।
अनेकजन्म-संसिद्ध-स्ततो याति पराङ्गतिम् ॥ ४५ ॥

44. By that very previous practice he is irresistibly carried away. Even a mere inquirer after Yoga transcends the Vedas.

45. Verily, a Yogi who practises assiduously, being purified by all sins, is perfected through many births, (and) then attains the supreme Goal.

SRIMAD-BHAGAVAD-GITA

तपस्विभ्योऽधिको योगी ज्ञानिभ्योऽपि मतोऽधिकः ।
कर्मिभ्यश्चाधिको योगी तस्मा-द्योगी-भवार्जुन ॥४६॥

योगिनामपि सर्वेषां मद्गतेनान्तरात्मना ।
श्रद्धावान् भजते यो मां स मे युक्त-तमो मतः ॥४७॥

इति श्रीमद्भगवद्गीतासूपनिषत्सु ब्रह्मविद्यायां योगशास्त्रे
श्रीकृष्णार्जुनसंवादे ध्यानयोगो नाम
षष्ठोऽध्यायः ॥

46. The Yogi is regarded as greater than ascetics, greater than even men of knowledge and greater also than those devoted to work; therefore be a Yogi, O Arjuna.

47. Of all Yogis even, he who, possessed of faith, worships Me with his mind absorbed in Me, is in My opinion the greatest.

॥ सप्तमोऽध्यायः ॥

(ज्ञानविज्ञानयोगः)

श्री भगवानुवाच —

मय्यासक्त-मनाः पार्थ योगं युञ्जन् मदाश्रयः ।
असंशयं समग्रं मां यथा ज्ञास्यसि तच्छृणु ॥ १ ॥

CHAPTER VII
THE WAY OF KNOWLEDGE AND REALIZATION

The Blessed Lord said:

1. Listen how, with the mind intent on Me, taking refuge in Me, and practising Yoga, O Pārtha (Arjuna), you will know Me in full, free from doubt.

SRIMAD-BHAGAVAD-GITA

ज्ञानं तेऽहं सविज्ञान-मिदं वक्ष्या-म्यशेषतः ।
यज्ज्ञात्वा नेह भूयोऽन्य-ज्ज्ञातव्य-मवशिष्यते ॥२॥

मनुष्याणां सहस्रेषु कश्चि-द्यतति सिद्धये ।
यततामपि सिद्धानां कश्चिन्मां वेत्ति तत्त्वतः ॥ ३ ॥

2. I shall tell you without reserve about this knowledge (Jnāna) together with realization (Vijnāna), knowing which there remains nothing further to be known here.

3. Among thousands of men one perchance struggles for perfection; even amongst those that struggle (one perchance becomes perfect), and even amongst those that are perfect, one perchance knows Me in reality.

भूमि-रापोऽनलो वायुः खं मनो बुद्धिरेव च ।
अहङ्कार इतीयं मे भिन्ना प्रकृति-रष्टधा ॥ ४ ॥

अपरेय-मितस्त्वन्यां प्रकृतिं विद्धि मे पराम् ।
जीव-भूतां महाबाहो ययेदं धार्यते जगत् ॥ ५ ॥

4. Earth, water, fire, air, ether, mind, intellect and egoism—thus is My Prakriti (Nature) divided into eight categories.

5. This is My lower Prakriti; different from this, O mighty-armed one, know that higher Prakriti of Mine in the form of the individual soul (Jiva) by which this world is sustained.

SRIMAD-BHAGAVAD-GITA

एतद्योनीनि भूतानि सर्वाणी-त्युपधारय ।
अहं कृत्स्नस्य जगतः प्रभवः प्रलय-स्तथा ॥ ६॥

मत्तः परतरं नान्यत् किंचिदस्ति धनञ्जय ।
मयि सर्वमिदं प्रोतं सूत्रे मणि-गणा इव ॥ ७ ॥

6. Know that all beings have these two for their origin; I am the origin of the entire universe as also its destroyer.

7. Higher than Myself there is nothing else, O Dhananjaya (Arjuna). In Me all this is strung like gems in a string.

THE WAY OF KNOWLEDGE AND REALIZATION 153

रसोऽह-मप्सु कौन्तेय प्रभास्मि शशि-सूर्ययोः ।
प्रणवः सर्ववेदेषु शब्दः खे पौरुषं नृषु ॥ ८ ॥

पुण्यो गन्धः पृथिव्यां च तेज-श्चास्मि विभावसौ ।
जीवनं सर्वभूतेषु तप-श्चास्मि तपस्विषु ॥ ९ ॥

8. I am, O son of Kunti, sapidity in water, lustre in the moon and the sun, the syllable Om in all the Vedas, sound in ether and enterprise in man.

9. I am pure odour in earth, brightness in fire, life in all beings and austerity in the ascetics.

SRIMAD-BHAGAVAD-GITA

बीजं मां सर्व-भूतानां विद्धि पार्थ सनातनम् ।
बुद्धि-बुद्धिमता-मस्मि तेज-स्तेजस्विना-महम् ॥१०॥

बलं बलवता-मस्मि काम-राग-विवर्जितम् ।
धर्माविरुद्धो भूतेषु कामोऽस्मि भरतर्षभ ॥ ११ ॥

10. Know me, O Pārtha, to be the eternal seed of all beings. I am the intelligence of the intelligent and the prowess of the powerful.

11. I am the strength of the strong, free from passion and attachment, and, O best of the Bharatas (Arjuna), I am that passion in people which is unopposed to one's duty (Dharma).

ये चैव सात्त्विका-भावा राजसा-स्तामसाश्च ये ।
मत्त एवेति तान्विद्धि न त्वहं तेषु ते मयि ॥ १२ ॥

त्रिभि-र्गुणमयै-र्भावै-रेभिः सर्व-मिदं जगत् ।
मोहितं नाभिजानाति मामेभ्यः पर-मव्ययम् ॥ १३ ॥

12. All those Sātvika (serene), Rājasika (active), and Tāmasika (passive) states that are there—know them to be born of Me alone; but I am not in them, (though) they abide in Me.

13. All this world, deluded by these three states composed of the Gunas, does not know Me, who am beyond these and immutable.

SRIMAD-BHAGAVAD-GITA

दैवी ह्येषा गुणमयी मम माया दुरत्यया ।
मामेव ये प्रपद्यन्ते माया-मेतां तरन्ति ते ॥ १४ ॥

न मां दुष्कृतिनो मूढाः प्रपद्यन्ते नराधमाः ।
माययापहृत-ज्ञाना आसुरं भाव-माश्रिताः ॥ १५ ॥

14. This divine illusion of Mine, constituted of the Gunas, is indeed hard to surmount; those who take refuge in Me alone, get over this illusion.

15. Wretches among men, the wicked and the ignorant do not take refuge in Me, being deprived of discrimination by Māyā, and betaking themselves to demoniac attitude.

THE WAY OF KNOWLEDGE AND REALIZATION 157

चतु-र्विधा भजन्ते मां जनाः सुकृतिनोऽर्जुन ।
आर्तो जिज्ञासु-रर्थार्थी ज्ञानी च भरतर्षभ ॥ १६ ॥
तेषां ज्ञानी नित्ययुक्त एकभक्ति-र्विशिष्यते ।
प्रियो हि ज्ञानिनोऽत्यर्थ-महं स च मम प्रियः ॥१७॥

16. Four kinds of people who have done virtuous deeds worship Me, O Arjuna—the distressed person, the aspirant after knowledge, the seeker of wealth and the man of knowledge, O best of Bharatas.

17. Of these, the man of knowledge who is constantly in communion and singleminded in devotion excels. To the man of knowledge I am very dear indeed, and he is dear to Me.

SRIMAD-BHAGAVAD-GITA

उदाराः सर्व एवैते ज्ञानी त्वात्मैव मे मतम् ।
आस्थितः स हि युक्तात्मा मामेवानुत्तमां गतिम् ॥१८॥

बहूनां जन्मना-मन्ते ज्ञानवान् मां प्रपद्यते ।
वासुदेवः सर्वमिति स महात्मा सुदुर्लभः ॥ १९ ॥

18. All of these are indeed noble, but the man of realization I regard as My very Self; for with his mind fixed (on Me), he has taken refuge in Me alone as the highest goal.

19. At the end of innumerable births, the man of realization takes refuge in Me, knowing that all this is Vāsudeva. Such a saint is exceedingly rare.

THE WAY OF KNOWLEDGE AND REALIZATION

कामैस्तैस्तैर्हृतज्ञानाः प्रपद्यन्तेऽन्यदेवताः ।
तं तं नियम-मास्थाय प्रकृत्या नियताः स्वया ॥२०॥

यो यो यां यां तनुं भक्तः श्रद्धयार्चितु-मिच्छति ।
तस्य तस्याचलां श्रद्धां तामेव विदधा-म्यहम् ॥२१॥

20. Deprived of discrimination by particular desires, they worship other deities observing particular rites, being swayed by their own nature.

21. Whatever form a particular devotee wishes to worship with faith—concerning that alone I make his faith unflinching.

SRIMAD-BHAGAVAD-GITA

स तया श्रद्धया युक्त-स्तस्याराधन-मीहते ।
लभते च ततः कामान् मयैव विहितान् हि तान् ॥ २२ ॥

अन्तवत्तु फलं तेषां तद्भव-त्यल्पमेधसाम् ।
देवान् देवयजो यान्ति मद्भक्ता यान्ति मामपि ॥ २३ ॥

22. Endowed with that faith, he worships that deity,
and from him gets his desires, which are indeed granted by
Me alone.

23. But that fruit of these men of little understanding
has an end; the worshippers of gods go to the gods, (but)
My devotees come to Me.

अव्यक्तं व्यक्ति-मापन्नं मन्यन्ते मामबुद्धयः ।
परं भाव-मजानन्तो ममाव्यय-मनुत्तमम् ॥ २४ ॥

नाहं प्रकाशः सर्वस्य योगमाया-समावृतः ।
मूढोऽयं नाभिजानाति लोको मामज-मव्ययम् ॥२५॥

24. Not knowing My immutable, unsurpassed supreme nature, the ignorant regard Me, the unmanifest, as coming into being.

25. I am not manifest to all, being veiled by My mysterious power (Yoga-māyā). This ignorant world does not know Me, the unborn and immutable.

SRIMAD-BHAGAVAD-GITA

वेदाहं समतीतानि वर्तमानानि चार्जुन ।
भविष्याणि च भूतानि मां तु वेद न कश्चन ॥२६॥

इच्छा-द्वेष-समुत्थेन द्वन्द्व-मोहेन भारत ।
सर्वभूतानि संमोहं सर्गे यान्ति परंतप ॥ २७ ॥

26. I know, O Arjuna, all beings past, present and future, but nobody knows Me.

27. All beings, O scorcher of foes, are deluded at birth by that deception due to the pairs of opposites which arises out of desire and aversion, O descendant of Bharata.

येषां त्वन्तगतं पापं जनानां पुण्य-कर्मणाम् ।
ते द्वन्द्व-मोह-निर्मुक्ता भजन्ते मां दृढव्रताः ॥२८॥

जरा-मरण-मोक्षाय मामाश्रित्य यतन्ति ये ।
ते ब्रह्म तद्विदुः कृत्स्न-मध्यात्मं कर्म चाखिलम् ॥२९॥

28. But those of virtuous actions whose sins have been at an end, are freed from the delusion of the dualities and worship Me with firmness of vow.

29. Those who strive for freedom from decay and death, taking refuge in Me, know that Brahman, all about the embodied self and action in its entirety.

SRIMAD-BHAGAVAD-GITA

साधिभूताधिदैवं मां साधियज्ञं च ये विदुः ।

प्रयाण-कालेऽपि च मां ते विदु-युक्त-चेतसः ॥३०॥

इति श्रीमद्भगवद्गीतासूपनिषत्सु ब्रह्मविद्यायां योगशास्त्रे

श्रीकृष्णार्जुनसंवादे ज्ञानविज्ञानयोगो नाम

सप्तमोऽध्यायः ॥

30. Those who know Me together with what concerns beings, the gods and sacrifices—fix their mind (on Me) and know Me even at the time of death.

॥ अष्टमोऽध्यायः ॥

(अक्षरब्रह्मयोगः)

अर्जुन उवाच—

किं तद्ब्रह्म किमध्यात्मं किं कर्म पुरुषोत्तम ।
अधिभूतं च किं प्रोक्त-मधिदैवं किमुच्यते ॥ १ ॥

CHAPTER VIII
THE WAY TO THE SUPREME SPIRIT

Arjuna said:

1. What is that Brahman, what is Adhyātma, and what is action, O best of men? What is called the Adhibhuta and what is said to be the Adhidaiva?

SRIMAD-BHAGAVAD-GITA

अधियज्ञः कथं कोऽत्र देहेऽस्मिन् मधुसूदन ।
प्रयाणकाले च कथं ज्ञेयोऽसि नियतात्मभिः ॥ २ ॥
श्रीभगवानुवाच—
अक्षरं ब्रह्म परमं स्वभावोऽध्यात्म-मुच्यते ।
भूतभावोद्भवकरो विसर्गः कर्मसंज्ञितः ॥ ३ ॥

2. Who and how is the Adhiyajna in this body,
O slayer of Madhu (Sri Krishna)? And how are You
known at the time of death by the self-restrained?

The Blessed Lord said:

3. The highest imperishable principle is Brahman.
Its existence as the embodied soul is called Adhyātma, and
the offering (into the sacrificial fire) which causes the origin
and development of beings is called action.

अधिभूतं क्षरो भावः पुरुषश्चाधिदैवतम् ।
अधियज्ञोऽहमेवात्र देहे देहभृतां वर ॥ ४ ॥

अन्तकाले च मामेव स्मरन् मुक्त्वा कलेवरम् ।
यः प्रयाति स मद्भावं याति नास्त्यत्र संशयः ॥५॥

4. Perishable entities are called Adhibhuta, the cosmic Being is called Adhidaiva, and I Myself am called the Adhiyajna in this body, O best of embodied beings.

5. He who at the time of death remembers Me alone and passes out, leaving the body, attains My being—there is no doubt about this.

SRIMAD-BHAGAVAD-GITA

यं यं वापि स्मरन् भावं त्यजत्यन्ते कलेवरम् ।
तं तमेवैति कौन्तेय सदा तद्भाव-भावितः ॥ ६ ॥

तस्मात् सर्वेषु कालेषु मामनुस्मर युध्य च ।
मय्यर्पित-मनो-बुद्धि-मामेवैष्य-स्यसंशयः ॥ ७ ॥

6. Thinking of whatever object at the time of death a person leaves the body, he attains, O son of Kunti, that very object, being constantly absorbed in its thought.

7. Therefore remember Me at all times and fight; with your mind and intellect devoted to Me, shall attain Me alone—there is no doubt about this.

अभ्यास-योग-युक्तेन चेतसा नान्य-गामिना ।
परमं पुरुषं दिव्यं याति पार्थानुचिन्तयन् ॥ ८ ॥

कविं पुराण-मनुशासितार-मणो-रणीयांस-मनुस्मरेद्यः ।
सर्वस्य धातार-मचिन्त्यरूप-मादित्यवर्णं तमसः परस्तात् ॥ ९ ॥

8. With a mind that has taken to the way of constant practice and does not stray to anything else, one who thinks of the supreme divine Being, attains Him, O Pārtha.

9-10. He who, endowed with devotion, meditates at the time of death with a steady mind, having by the power of Yoga properly fixed the life-breath in between the eye-

प्रयाणकाले मनसाचलेन भक्त्या युक्तो योगबलेन चैव ।
भ्रुवो-र्मध्ये प्राणमावेश्य सम्यक् स तं परं पुरुष-मुपैति दिव्यम् ॥

यदक्षरं वेदविदो वदन्ति विशन्ति यद्यतयो वीतरागाः ।
यदिच्छन्तो ब्रह्मचर्यं चरन्ति तत्ते पदं संग्रहेण प्रवक्ष्ये ॥११॥

brows, on the Being who is wise, ancient, the ruler, smaller than the smallest, the sustainer of all, inconceivable form, resplendent like the sun and beyond ignorance—he attains the shining supreme Being.

11. That imperishable Principle which the knowers of the Vedas describe, into which aspirants bereft of all desires enter, desiring which one lives the abstinent life of a student—that goal I shall tell you in brief.

सर्व-द्वाराणि संयम्य मनो हृदि निरुध्य च ।
मूर्ध्न्याधायात्मनः प्राण-मास्थितो योग-धारणाम् ॥१२॥

ओमित्येकाक्षरं ब्रह्म व्याहरन् मामनुस्मरन् ।
यः प्रयाति त्यजन् देहं स याति परमां गतिम् ॥१३॥

12-13. Controlling all the inlets (organs), confining the mind to the heart, fixing the life-breath in the head, betaking himself to absorption in Yoga, repeating the monosyllable Om, which is Brahman, and thinking of Me, he who departs leaving the body, attains the highest Goal.

SRIMAD-BHAGAVAD-GITA

अनन्य-चेताः सततं यो मां स्मरति नित्यशः ।
तस्याहं सुलभः पार्थ नित्य-युक्तस्य योगिनः ॥१४॥

मामुपेत्य पुनर्जन्म दुःखालय-मशाश्वतम् ।
नाप्नुवन्ति महात्मानः संसिद्धिं परमां गताः ॥१५॥

14. To the ever-restrained Yogi who constantly remembers Me every day with his mind on nothing else, O Pārtha, I am easily accessible.

15. The great-souled ones, having attained Me, have no more birth, which is the abode of misery and non-eternal, for they have attained the highest perfection.

आब्रह्म-भुवनाल्लोकाः पुनरावर्तिनोऽर्जुन ।
मामुपेत्य तु कौन्तेय पुनर्जन्म न विद्यते ॥ १६ ॥

सहस्रयुगपर्यन्त-महर्यद्ब्रह्मणो विदुः ।
रात्रिं युगसहस्रान्तां तेऽहोरात्र-विदो जनाः ॥ १७ ॥

16. All the worlds, O Arjuna, including the world of Brahmā are subject to recurrence, but after attaining Me there is no rebirth, O son of Kunti.

17. Those who know Brahmā's day that lasts for a thousand Yugas, are knowers of day and night.

SRIMAD-BHAGAVAD-GITA

अव्यक्ता-द्वयक्तयः सर्वाः प्रभवन्त्यहरागमे ।
रात्र्यागमे प्रलीयन्ते तत्रैवाव्यक्त-संज्ञके ॥ १८ ॥

भूतग्रामः स एवायं भूत्वा भूत्वा प्रलीयते ।
रात्र्यागमेऽवशः पार्थ प्रभव-त्यहरागमे ॥ १९ ॥

18. From the Unmanifest all manifested beings are born at the advent of (Brahmā's) day, and at the approach of (his) night they get merged in that very thing called the Unmanifest.

19. That very multitude of beings, being born again and again, is absorbed at the approach of night, O Pārtha, and at the approach of the day is born again in spite of itself.

परस्तस्मात्तु भावोऽन्योऽव्यक्तोऽव्यक्तात् सनातनः ।
यः स सर्वेषु भूतेषु नश्यत्सु न विनश्यति ॥ २० ॥

अव्यक्तोऽक्षर इत्युक्त-स्तमाहुः परमां गतिम् ।
यं प्राप्य न निवर्तन्ते तद्धाम परमं मम ॥ २१ ॥

20. Beyond this Unmanifest there is another unmanifest eternal Being that does not perish when all creatures perish.

21. That Unmanifest which is called the Imperishable is said to be the supreme Goal, attaining which they return not; that is My supreme abode (state).

SRIMAD-BHAGAVAD-GITA

पुरुषः स परः पार्थ भक्त्या लभ्य-स्त्वनन्यया ।
यस्यान्तःस्थानि भूतानि येन सर्वमिदं ततम् ॥२२॥

यत्र काले त्वनावृत्ति-मावृत्तिं चैव योगिनः ।
प्रयाता यान्ति तं कालं वक्ष्यामि भरतर्षभ ॥ २३ ॥

22. That supreme Being, O Pārtha, in whom are all
beings and by whom all this is pervaded, is attainable by
one-point devotion.

23. The time at which departing (from hence) the
Yogis attain non-return or return—that time, O best of
Bharatas, I shall tell you.

अग्नि ज्योति-रह: शुक्र: षण्मासा उत्तरायणम्।
तत्र प्रयाता गच्छन्ति ब्रह्म ब्रह्मविदो जनाः ॥२४॥
धूमो रात्रि-स्तथा कृष्णः षण्मासा दक्षिणायनम् ।
तत्र चान्द्रमसं ज्योति-र्योगी प्राप्य निवर्तते ॥ २५ ॥

24. Fire, the flame, the day, the bright half of the month and the six months of the sun's northern course—departing by this path the knowers of Brahman attain Brahman.

25. Smoke, the night, the dark half of the month, and the six months of the sun's southern passage—departing by this path the Yogi attains the lunar sphere and returns (thence).

SRIMAD-BHAGAVAD-GITA

शुक्लकृष्णे गती ह्येते जगतः शाश्वते मते ।
एकया यात्यनावृत्ति-मन्ययाऽवर्तते पुनः ॥ २६ ॥

नैते सृती पार्थ जानन् योगी मुह्यति कश्चन ।
तस्मात् सर्वेषु कालेषु योगयुक्तो भवार्जुन ॥ २७ ॥

26. These two paths of the world, the bright and the dark, are considered to be eternal; by one, one returns not, and by the other, one returns.

27. Knowing these paths, O Pārtha, no Yogi is deluded; therefore at all times, O Arjuna, be endowed with Yoga.

वेदेषु यज्ञेषु तपस्सु चैव दानेषु यत्पुण्यफलं प्रदिष्टम् ।
अत्येति तत्सर्व-मिदं विदित्वा योगी परं स्थान-मुपैति चाद्यम् ॥

इति श्रीमद्भगवद्गीतासूपनिषत्सु ब्रह्मविद्यायां योगशास्त्रे
श्रीकृष्णार्जुनसंवादे अक्षरब्रह्मयोगो नाम
अष्टमोऽध्यायः ॥

28. Whatever good result is declared regarding the Vedas, sacrifices, asceticism and gifts—all that the Yogi who knows the above transcends and attains the primeval supreme Abode.

|| नवमोऽध्यायः ||
(राजविद्याराजगुह्ययोगः)

श्री भगवानुवाच—

इदं तु ते गुह्य-तमं प्रवक्ष्या-म्यनसूयवे ।
ज्ञानं विज्ञान-सहितं यज्ज्ञात्वा मोक्ष्यसेऽशुभात् ॥१॥

Chapter IX

THF WAY OF ROYAL KNOWLEDGE AND ROYAL SECRET

The Blessed Lord said :

1. To you who are not cavilling, I shall teach this most secret knowledge in particular, coupled with realization, knowing which you will be freed from evil.

THE WAY OF ROYAL KNOWLEDGE AND ROYAL SECRET

राजविद्या राजगुह्यं पवित्र-मिद-मुत्तमम् ।
प्रत्यक्षावगमं धर्म्यं सुसुखं कर्तुं-मव्ययम् ॥२॥

अश्रद्दधानाः पुरुषा धर्मस्यास्य परंतप ।
अप्राप्य मां निवर्तन्ते मृत्यु-संसार-वर्त्मनि ॥ ३ ॥

2. This is royal knowledge, the royal secret, supremely holy, directly experienced, righteous, easy to practise and imperishable.

3. Persons wanting in faith in this teaching, O scorcher of foes, return to the path of this mortal world without attaining Me.

SRIMAD-BHAGAVAD-GITA

मया तत-मिदं सर्वं जग-द्व्यक्त-मूर्तिना ।
मत्स्थानि सर्व-भूतानि न चाहं तेष्ववस्थितः ॥ ४ ॥

न च मत्स्थानि भूतानि पश्य मे योग-मैश्वरम् ।
भूतभृन्न च भूतस्थो ममात्मा भूतभावनः ॥ ५ ॥

4. All this is pervaded by Me of unmanifest form; all beings are in me, but I am not in them.

5. Nor are the beings in Me, behold My divine mystery; (though) the sustainer and the protector of beings, yet, My Self is not in these beings.

यथाकाश-स्थितो नित्यं वायुः सर्वत्रगो महान् ।
तथा सर्वाणि भूतानि मत्स्थानीत्युपधारय ॥ ६ ॥

सर्वभूतानि कौन्तेय प्रकृतिं यान्ति मामिकाम् ।
कल्पक्षये पुनस्तानि कल्पादौ विसृजाम्यहम् ॥ ७ ॥

6. As the vast wind blowing everywhere ever abides in space, know, even so do all beings abide in Me.

7. At the end of a cycle all beings, O son of Kunti, attain My Prakriti; at the beginning of the (next) cycle I again send them forth.

SRIMAD-BHAGAVAD-GITA

प्रकृतिं स्वा-मवष्टभ्य विसृजामि पुनः पुनः ।
भूतग्राम-मिमं कृत्स्न-मवशं प्रकृते-र्वशात् ॥ ८ ॥

न च मां तानि कर्माणि निबध्नन्ति धनञ्जय ।
उदासीनव-दासीन-मसक्तं तेषु कर्मसु ॥ ९ ॥

8. Presiding over My Nature (Prakriti), I again and again send forth this entire aggregate of helpless beings, according to their nature.

9. These acts (of creation, etc.) do not bind Me, O Arjuna, who remain unattached to them like one indifferent.

मयाध्यक्षेण प्रकृतिः सूयते सचराचरम् ।
हेतुनानेन कौन्तेय जग-द्विपरिवर्तते ॥ १० ॥

अवजानन्ति मां मूढा मानुषीं तनु-माश्रितम् ।
परं भाव-मजानन्तो मम भूत-महेश्वरम् ॥ ११ ॥

10. Presided over by Me, Prakriti brings forth the world of moving and unmoving things; for this reason, O son of Kunti (Arjuna), the world revolves.

11. The ignorant deride Me who have taken a human form, not knowing My higher nature as the great Lord of beings.

SRIMAD-BHAGAVAD-GITA

मोघाशा मोघकर्माणो मोघज्ञाना विचेतसः ।
राक्षसीं-मासुरीं चैव प्रकृतिं मोहिनीं श्रिताः ॥ १२ ॥

महात्मानस्तु मां पार्थ दैवीं प्रकृति-माश्रिताः ।
भजन्त्यनन्य-मनसो ज्ञात्वा भूतादि-मव्ययम् ॥१३॥

12. Of vain hopes, of vain efforts, of vain knowledge, thoughtless and taking to the deceptive demoniac and fiendish nature (they deride Me).

13. But the great-souled ones taking to the divine nature, O Pārtha, worship Me with one-pointed devotion, knowing Me to be the cause of all beings and immutable.

सततं कीर्तयन्तो मां यतन्तश्च दृढव्रताः।
नमस्यन्तश्च मां भक्त्या नित्ययुक्ता उपासते॥ १४॥

ज्ञान-यज्ञेन चाप्यन्ये यजन्तो मामुपासते।
एकत्वेन पृथक्त्वेन बहुधा विश्वतोमुखम्॥ १५॥

14. Always praising Me, striving with austere vows, and bowing down to Me with devotion, always steadfast, they worship Me.

15. Worshipping through the knowledge-sacrifice others adore Me, either as identical or as separate, or they adore Me, the manifold, in different forms.

SRIMAD-BHAGAVAD-GITA

अहं ऋतु-रहं यज्ञः स्वधाह-मह-मौषधम् ।
मन्त्रोऽहमहमेवाज्य-महमग्नि-रहं हुतम् ॥ १६ ॥

पिताह-मस्य जगतो माता धाता पितामहः ।
वेद्यं पवित्र-मोङ्कार ऋक् साम यजुरेव च ॥ १७ ॥

16. I am Kratu, I am Yajna, I am the oblation to the Manes, I am the product of annuals, I am the Mantra, I alone am the clarified butter, I am the (sacrificial) fire and the offering in the fire.

17. I am the father of this world, the mother, the dispenser, the grandsire, that which is to be known, the purifier, the Om and also the Vedas—Rik, Sāman and Yajus.

THE WAY OF ROYAL KNOWLEDGE AND ROYAL SECRET 189

गति-भर्ता प्रभुः साक्षी निवासः शरणं सुहृत् ।
प्रभवः प्रलयः स्थानं निधानं बीज-मव्ययम् ॥ १८ ॥

तपाम्यह-महं वर्षं निगृह्णा-म्युत्सृजामि च ।
अमृतं चैव मृत्युश्च सदसच्चाह-मर्जुन ॥ १९ ॥

18. I am the goal, the sustainer, the Lord, the witness, the abode, the refuge, the friend, the source, the destroyer, the support, the repository and the eternal seed.

19. I give heat, I restrain and let loose the rain, I am immortality, I am death, I am manifest and unmanifest also, O Arjuna.

SRIMAD-BHAGAVAD-GITA

त्रैविद्या मां सोमपाः पूत-पापा यज्ञै-रिष्ट्वा स्वर्गतिं प्रार्थयन्ते ।
ते पुण्य-मासाद्य सुरेन्द्रलोक-मश्नन्ति दिव्यान् दिवि देवभोगान् ॥

ते तं भुक्त्वा स्वर्ग-लोकं विशालं क्षीणे पुण्ये मर्त्य-लोकं विशन्ति ।
एवं त्रयीधर्म-मनुप्रपन्ना गतागतं कामकामा लभन्ते ॥ २१ ॥

20. The knowers of the Vedas, purified from sins by drinking the Soma juice and worshipping Me with sacrifices, pray for access to heaven; they having attained the meritorious sphere of Indra, experience in heaven celestial enjoyments of the gods.

21. Having enjoyed the extensive heavenly sphere, when their virtue is exhausted, they enter the mortal world. Thus those who take refuge in the religion of the Vedas, desirous of enjoyments, go and come.

अनन्य-श्चिन्तयन्तो मां ये जनाः पर्युपासते ।
तेषां नित्याभियुक्तानां योगक्षेमं वहाम्यहम् ॥२२॥
येऽप्यन्य-देवता-भक्ता यजन्ते श्रद्धयान्विताः ।
तेऽपि मामेव कौन्तेय यजन्त्यविधि-पूर्वकम् ॥२३॥

22. Those persons, who think of nothing else and worship Me through meditation—the accession to and the maintenance of the welfare of such ever devout person I look after.

23. Even those devotees of other gods who worship (them) endowed with faith, worship Me alone, O son of Kunti (Arjuna), though in an unauthorized way.

SRIMAD-BHAGAVAD-GITA

अहं हि सर्व-यज्ञानां भोक्ता च प्रभुरेव च ।
न तु मामभिजानन्ति तत्त्वेनात-श्च्यवन्ति ते ॥ २४ ॥
यान्ति देव-व्रता देवान् पितॄन् यान्ति पितृ-व्रताः ।
भूतानि यान्ति भूतेज्या यान्ति मद्याजिनोऽपि माम् ॥ २५ ॥

24. I am the enjoyer, and the Lord also, of all sacrifices. But they do not know Me in truth; thereore they fall down.

25. The worshippers of the gods go to the gods, the worshippers of the maner go to the manes, the worshippers of the spirits go to the spirits, and My worshippers too come to me.

पत्रं पुष्पं फलं तोयं यो मे भक्त्या प्रयच्छति।
तदहं भक्त्युपहृत-मश्नामि प्रयतात्मनः॥ २६॥

यत्करोषि यदश्नासि यज्जुहोषि ददासि यत्।
यत्तपस्यसि कौन्तेय तत्कुरुष्व मदर्पणम्॥ २७॥

26. He who with devotion offers Me a leaf, a flower, a fruit or water, that devout offering of the pure-minded one I accept.

27. Whatever you do, or eat, or sacrifice, or give, whatever austerity you perform, that, O son of Kunti, offer unto Me.

SRIMAD-BHAGAVAD-GITA

शुभाशुभ-फलै-रेवं मोक्ष्यसे कर्मबन्धनैः ।
सन्न्यासयोग-युक्तात्मा विमुक्तो मामुपैष्यसि ॥ २८॥

समोऽहं सर्वभूतेषु न मे द्वेष्योऽस्ति न प्रियः ।
ये भजन्ति तु मां भक्त्या मयि ते तेषु चाप्यहम् ॥२९॥

28. Thus you will be rid of the bonds of action resulting in good and evil; being free and with your mind endowed with the Yoga of renunciation, you will attain **Me**.

29. I am the same to all beings; there is no **one** hateful or dear to Me: but they who worship Me **with** devotion, are in Me, and I am also in them.

अपि चेत् सुदुराचारो भजते मामनन्यभाक् ।
साधुरेव स मन्तव्यः सम्यग्व्यवसितो हि सः ॥३०॥

क्षिप्रं भवति धर्मात्मा शश्वच्छान्तिं निगच्छति ।
कौन्तेय प्रतिजानीहि न मे भक्तः प्रणश्यति ॥३१॥

30. Even if a very wicked person worships Me to the exclusion of anybody else, he should be regarded as righteous, for he has rightly resolved.

31. He soon becomes righteous-minded and attains eternal peace: O Son of Kunti, proclaim (to the world) that My devotee never perishes.

SRIMAD-BHAGAVAD-GITA

मां हि पार्थ व्यपाश्रित्य येऽपि स्युः पाप-योनयः ।
स्त्रियो वैश्या-स्तथा शूद्रा-स्तेऽपि यान्ति परां गतिम् ॥

किं पुनर्ब्राह्मणाः पुण्या भक्ता राजर्षय-स्तथा ।
अनित्य-मसुखं लोक-मिमं प्राप्य भजस्व माम् ॥ ३३ ॥

32. Even they who are of sinful birth, women, Vaishyas, as also Sūdras, taking refuge in Me, verily attain the highest goal.

33. Not to mention virtuous Brāhmanas and devoted royal sages. Having attained this ephemeral joyless body, worship Me.

THE WAY OF ROYAL KNOWLEDGE AND ROYAL SECRET

मन्मना भव मद्भक्तो मद्याजी मां नमस्कुरु ।
मामेवैष्यसि युक्त्वैवं-मात्मानं मत्परायणः ॥ ३४ ॥

इति श्रीमद्भगवद्गीतासूपनिषत्सु ब्रह्मविद्यायां योगशास्त्रे
श्रीकृष्णार्जुनसंवादे राजविद्याराजगुह्ययोगो नाम
नवमोऽध्यायः ॥

34. Fix your mind on Me, be My devotee, sacrifice to Me; thus fixing the mind on Me and having Me for the supreme goal, you will attain Me alone.

14.
———

॥ दशमोऽध्यायः ॥

(विभूतियोगः)

श्री भगवानुवाच—

भूय एव महाबाहो श्रृणु मे परमं वचः ।
यत्तेऽहं प्रीयमाणाय वक्ष्यामि हित-काम्यया ॥ १ ॥

Chapter X
MEDITATION ON THE DIVINE GLORIES

The Blessed Lord said:

1. Hear again, O Mighty-armed one, My supreme word, which I, wishing your welfare, shall tell you who take delight in it.

MEDITATION ON THE DIVINE GLORIES

न मे विदुः सुरगणाः प्रभवं न महर्षयः ।
अहमादिर्हि देवानां महर्षीणां च सर्वशः ॥ २ ॥

यो मामज-मनादिं च वेत्ति लोक-महेश्वरम् ।
असंमूढः स मर्त्येषु सर्व-पापैः प्रमुच्यते ॥ ३ ॥

2. Neither the gods nor the great sages know My birth; for I am the cause of the gods and the great sages in all respects.

3. He who knows Me, the birthless and beginningless Lord of creatures, is undeluded among men and is freed from all sins.

SRIMAD-BHAGAVAD-GITA

बुद्धि-ज्ञान-मसंमोहः क्षमा सत्यं दमः शमः ।
सुखं दुखं भवोऽभावो भयं चाभयमेव च ॥ ४ ॥

अहिंसा समता तुष्टि-स्तपो दानं यशोऽयशः ।
भवन्ति भावा भूतानां मत्त एव पृथग्विधाः ॥ ५ ॥

4-5. Discrimination, knowledge, nondelusion, forgiveness, truthfulness, selfcontrol, tranquility, happiness, misery, existence, non-existence, fear and also fearlessness, non-injury, equanimity, contentment, austerity, charity, fame, ill-fame—these different dispositions of beings are indeed born of Me.

महर्षयः सप्त पूर्वे चत्वारो मनवस्तथा ।
मद्भावा मानसा जाता येषां लोक इमाः प्रजाः ॥६॥

एतां विभूतिं योगं च मम यो वेत्ति तत्त्वतः ।
सोऽविकम्पेन योगेन युज्यते नात्र संशयः ॥ ७ ॥

6. The seven great sages, the earlier four, and also the Manus, were born of My mind endowed with My essence—whose progeny are these in the world.

7. He who knows in truth this glory and power of Mine, attains unflinching Yoga: there is no doubt about this.

SRIMAD-BHAGAVAD-GITA

अहं सर्वस्य प्रभवो मत्तः सर्वं प्रवर्तते ।
इति मत्वा भजन्ते मां बुधा भाव-समन्विताः ॥ ८ ॥

मच्चित्ता मद्गत-प्राणा बोधयन्तः परस्परम् ।
कथयन्तश्च मां नित्यं तुष्यन्ति च रमन्ति च ॥९॥

8. I am the source of all, everything is produced out of Me, knowing thus the wise worship Me with devotion.

9. With their mind and senses directed to Me, explaining Me to each other, and talking of Me—they are always pleased and happy.

MEDITATION ON THE DIVINE GLORIES

तेषां सतत-युक्तानां भजतां प्रीति-पूर्वकम् ।
ददामि बुद्धि-योगं तं येन मामुपयान्ति ते ॥१०॥

तेषामेवानुकम्पार्थ-मह-मज्ञानजं तमः ।
नाशया-म्यात्मभावस्थो ज्ञान-दीपेन भास्वता ॥११॥

10. To these who are (thus) ever devoted to Me and worship Me with love, I give that Yoga of understanding by which they come unto Me.

11. Just to bless them, I, residing in their intellect, destroy the darkness born of ignorance by the resplendent light of knowledge.

SRIMAD-BHAGAVAD-GITA

अर्जुन उवाच—

परं ब्रह्म परं धाम पवित्रं परमं भवान् ।
पुरुषं शाश्वतं दिव्य-मादिदेव-मजं विभुम् ॥ १२ ॥

आहुस्त्वा-मृषयः सर्वे देवर्षि-र्नारद-स्तथा ।
असितो देवलो व्यासः स्वयं चैव ब्रवीषि मे ॥१३॥

Arjuna said :

12-13. You are the supreme Brahman, the supreme
abode and extremely holy. All sages, the divine sage
Nārada, (as also) Asita, Devala and Vyāsa call You the
eternal, resplendent Being, the primeval Deity, birthless
and omnipresent. And you too are telling me so.

सर्वमेत-द्दतं मन्ये यन्मां वदसि केशव ।
न हि ते भगवन् व्यक्तिं विदुर्देवा न दानवाः ॥१४॥

स्वयमेवात्मनात्मानं वेत्थ त्वं पुरुषोत्तम ।
भूतभावन भूतेश देवदेव जगत्पते ॥ १५ ॥

14. All this and what (else) You say unto me, O Kesava, I regard as true; O Lord, verily, neither the gods nor the demons know Your manifestations.

15. You alone know Yourself by yourself, O best of persons, O creator of beings, O Lord of beings, O God of gods, O Lord of the universe.

SRIMAD-BHAGAVAD-GITA

वक्तुमर्हस्यशेषेण दिव्या ह्यात्म-विभूतयः ।
याभि-र्विभूतिभि-र्लोका-निमांस्त्वं व्याप्य तिष्ठसि ॥१६॥

कथं विद्या-महं योगिस्त्वां सदा परिचिन्तयन् ।
केषु केषु च भावेषु चिन्त्योऽसि भगवन् मया ॥१७॥

16. Verily, You alone can fully tell about Your divine glories, through which pervading all these worlds You exist.

17. In what ways always thinking of You, O Yogin, can I know You? In which particular objects are You to be meditated upon by me?

MEDITATION ON THE DIVINE GLORIES

विस्तरेणात्मनो योगं विभूतिं च जनार्दन ।
भूयः कथय तृप्तिर्हि शृण्वतो नास्ति मेऽमृतम् ॥१८॥

श्रीभगवानुवाच—
हन्त ते कथयिष्यामि दिव्या ह्यात्म-विभूतयः ।
प्राधान्यतः कुरुश्रेष्ठ नास्त्यन्तो विस्तरस्य मे ॥१९॥

18. O Janārdana, tell me once more in detail about Your powers and glories; for I am not satiated by listening to Your nectarlike words.

The Blessed Lord said:

19. All right, I shall tell you about My principal divine glories, O best of the Kurus (Arjuna); for there is no end to the details of My glories.

SRIMAD-BHAGAVAD-GITA

अहमात्मा गुडाकेश सर्वभूताशय-स्थितः ।
अह-मादिश्च मध्यं च भूताना-मन्त एव च ॥ २० ॥

आदित्याना-महं विष्णु-ज्योतिषां रवि-रंशुमान् ।
मरीचि-मरुता-मस्मि नक्षत्राणा-महं शशी ॥ २१ ॥

20. I am, O Gudākesha, the Self residing in the minds of all creatures ; I am the beginning, the middle and also the end of beings.

21. Of the Ādityas I am Vishnu, of luminaries I am the radiant sun, of the Maruts I am Marichi, and among constellations I am the moon.

वेदानां सामवेदोऽस्मि देवाना-मस्मि वासवः ।
इन्द्रियाणां मनश्चास्मि भूताना-मस्मि चेतना ॥२२॥

रुद्राणां शङ्करश्चास्मि वित्तेशो यक्ष-रक्षसाम् ।
वसूनां पावक-श्चास्मि मेरुः शिखरिणा-महम् ॥२३॥

22. Of the Vedas I am the Sāma Veda, of the gods I am Indra, of the senses I am the mind, and in beings I am consciousness.

23. Of the Rudras I am Sankara, of the Yakshas and Rakshasas I am Kubera, of the Vasus I am Fire, and among mountains I am Meru.

पुरोधसां च मुख्यं मां विद्धि पार्थ बृहस्पतिम् ।
सेनानीना-महं स्कन्दः सरसा-मस्मि सागरः ॥२४॥

महर्षीणां भृगु-रहं गिरा-मस्म्येक मक्षरम् ।
यज्ञानां जप-यज्ञोऽस्मि स्थावराणां हिमालयः ॥२५॥

24. Know that I am Brihaspati, the foremost among priests, O Pārtha : of army leaders I am Skanda, of natural reservoirs I am the ocean.

25. Of the great sages I am Bhrigu, of words I am the monosyllable (Om), of sacrifices I am the Japa sacrifice, of immovables I am the Himālayas.

MEDITATION ON THE DIVINE GLORIES

अश्वत्थः सर्ववृक्षाणां देवर्षीणां च नारदः ।
गन्धर्वाणां चित्ररथः सिद्धानां कपिलो मुनिः ॥२६॥

उच्चैःश्रवस-मश्वानां विद्धि माममृतोद्भवम् ।
ऐरावतं गजेन्द्राणां नराणां च नराधिपम् ॥ २७ ॥

26. Of all trees I am the Ashvattha (peepul tree), of divine sages I am Nārada, of Gandharvas I am Chitraratha, and amongst perfect souls I am the saint Kapila.

27. Of horses know Me to be Uchchaiḥshravas born of (the churning for) nectar, of lordly elephants Airāvata, and amongst men the king.

SRIMAD-BHAGAVAD-GITA

आयुधाना-महं वज्रं धेनूना-मस्मि कामधुक् ।
प्रजनश्चास्मि कन्दर्पः सर्पाणा-मस्मि वासुकिः ॥ २८ ॥

अनन्तश्चास्मि नागानां वरुणो यादसामहम् ।
पितृणामर्यमा चास्मि यमः संयमता-महम् ॥२९॥

28. Of weapons I am the thunderbolt, of cows I am the Kāmadhenu, I am the productive passion, and of poisonous serpents l am Vāsuki.

29. Among non-poisonous snakes I am Ananta, of acquatic beings I am Varuna, of the manes I am Aryaman, of regulators I am Yama.

प्रह्लादश्चास्मि दैत्यानां कालः कलयता-महम् ।
मृगाणां च मृगेन्द्रोऽहं वैनतेयश्च पक्षिणाम् ॥ ३० ॥

पवनः पवतामस्मि रामः शस्त्रभृता-महम् ।
झषाणां मकरश्चास्मि स्रोतसामस्मि जाह्नवी ॥ ३१ ॥

30. Of demons I am Prahlāda, of reckoners I am time, among beasts I am the lion, and among birds I am Garuda.

31. I am the wind among those who move fast, of wielders of weapons I am Rāma, among fish I am the Makara, of rivers I am the Gangā.

SRIMAD-BHAGAVAD-GITA

सर्गाणा-मादि-रन्तश्च मध्यं चैवाह-मर्जुन ।
अध्यात्मविद्या विद्यानां वादः प्रवदता-महम् ॥३२॥

अक्षराणा-मकारोऽस्मि द्वन्द्वः सामासिकस्य च ।
अहमेवाक्षयः कालो धाताहं विश्वतो-मुखः ॥ ३३ ॥

32. Of creations I am the beginning, the end, as also the middle, O Arjuna; of sciences I am metaphysics, and I am the constructive reasoning of the controversialists.

33. Of letters I am the letter A and of compounds I am the Dvandva; I Myself am eternal time, I am the universal dispenser.

मृत्युः सर्वहरश्चाह-मुद्भवश्च भविष्यताम् ।
कीर्तिः श्रीर्वाक्च नारीणां स्मृति-र्मेधा धृतिः क्षमा ॥ ३४ ॥
बृहत्साम तथा साम्नां गायत्री छन्दसा-महम् ।
मासानां मार्गशीर्षोऽह-मृतूनां कुसुमाकरः ॥ ३५ ॥

34. I am the all-destroying death, the prosperity of potentially prosperous beings, amongst women I am fame, prosperity, speech, memory, intelligence, fortitude and forgiveness.

35. Of the Vedic lyrics also I am the Brihat Sāma, of metres I am the Gāyatri, of months I am the Agrahāyana, of seasons I am the spring.

SRIMAD-BHAGAVAD-GITA

द्यूतं छलयता-मस्मि तेज-स्तेजस्विना-महम् ।
जयोऽस्मि व्यवसायोऽस्मि सत्त्वं सत्त्ववता-महम् ॥३६॥

वृष्णीनां वासुदेवोऽस्मि पाण्डवानां धनञ्जयः ।
मुनीनामप्यहं व्यासः कवीना-मुशना कविः ॥३७॥

36. Of those who deceive I am gambling, I am the
prowess of the powerful, I am victory, I am effort, and I am
the goodness of the good.

37. Of the Vrishnis I am Vāsudeva, of the Pāndavas
I am Dhananjaya (Arjuna), of sages I am Vyāsa, of seers
I am the seer Ushanas.

दण्डो दमयता-मस्मि नीति-रस्मि जिगीषताम् ।
मौनं चैवास्मि गुह्यानां ज्ञानं ज्ञानवता-महम् ॥३८॥

यच्चापि सर्वभूतानां बीजं तदह-मर्जुन ।
न तदस्ति विना यत्स्यान्मया भूतं चराचरम् ॥३९॥

38. Of punishers I am the rod, of those desirous of victory I am policy, of secrets also I am silence, I am the knowledge of the wise.

39. I am also, O Arjuna, that which is the germ of all beings; there is no being, moving or stationary, which can exist without Me.

SRIMAD-BHAGAVAD-GITA

नान्तोऽस्ति मम दिव्यानां विभूतीनां परंतप ।
एष तूद्देशतः प्रोक्तो विभूते-र्विस्तरो मया ॥४०॥

यद्यद्विभूतिमत् सत्त्वं श्रीम-दूर्जित-मेव वा ।
तत्तदेवावगच्छ त्वं मम तेजोंश-संभवम् ॥ ४१ ॥

40. O tormentor of foes. there is no end to My divine glories; these details of My glories I have only stated in brief.

41. Whatever thing is glorious, excellent or pre-eminent, verily, know that is born of a portion of My splendour.

MEDITATION ON THE DIVINE GLORIES

अथवा बहुनैतेन किं ज्ञातेन तवार्जुन ।
विष्टभ्याहमिदं कृत्स्न-मेकांशेन स्थितो जगत् ॥४२॥

इति श्रीमद्भगवद्गीतासूपनिषत्सु ब्रह्मविद्यायां योगशास्त्रे
श्रीकृष्णार्जुनसंवादे विभूतियोगो नाम
दशमोऽध्यायः ॥

42. But of what avail is it to you to know all these details; I exist pervading this entire universe by a portion of Myself.

॥ एकादशोऽध्यायः ॥

(विश्वरूपदर्शनयोगः)

अर्जुन उवाच—

मदनुग्रहाय परमं गुह्य-मध्यात्म-संज्ञितम् ।
यत्त्वयोक्तं वचस्तेन मोहोऽयं विगतो मम ॥ १ ॥

Chapter XI

THE VISION OF THE UNIVERSAL FORM

Arjuna Said:

1. By the supreme and secret discourse known as Adhyātma that You have delivered for favouring me, this delusion of mine has been destroyed.

भवाप्ययौ हि भूतानां श्रुतौ विस्तरशो मया ।
त्वत्तः कमलपत्राक्ष माहात्म्य-मपि चाव्ययम् ॥२॥

एवमेत-द्यथात्थ त्वमात्मानं परमेश्वर ।
द्रष्टु-मिच्छामि ते रूप-मैश्वरं पुरुषोत्तम ॥ ३ ॥

2. Verily, about the origin and dissolution of beings I have heard from You in detail, as also, O Lotus-eyed one, about Your inexhaustible greatness.

3. What You say about Yourself, O great Lord, is just so; O best of persons, I desire to see Your Divine form.

मन्यसे यदि तच्छक्यं मया द्रष्टुमिति प्रभो ।
योगेश्वर ततो मे त्वं दर्शयात्मानमव्ययम् ॥ ४

श्री भगवानुवाच—

पश्य मे पार्थ रूपाणि शतशोऽथ सहस्रशः ।
नानाविधानि दिव्यानि नानावर्णाकृतीनि च ॥ ५ ॥

4. O Lord, if You think that (form of Yours) can be seen by me, then, O Lord of Yogis, show me Your eternal Self.

The Blessed Lord said:

5. See My various divine forms, O Pārtha, of diverse hues and shapes, by the hundreds and thousands.

THE VISION OF THE UNIVERSAL FORM

पश्यादित्यान् वसून् रुद्रान्अश्विनौ मरुतस्तथा ।
बहून्यदृष्टपूर्वाणि पश्याश्चर्याणि भारत ॥ ६ ॥

इहैकस्थं जगत्कृत्स्नं पश्याद्य सचराचरम् ।
मम देहे गुडाकेश यच्चान्यद्-द्रष्टु-मिच्छसि ॥ ७ ॥

6. See the Ādityas, the Vasus, the Rudras, the two Asvins and the Maruts; see many wonderful (forms) never seen before, O descendant of Bharata.

7. See this day the entire universe with movable and immovable objects united here in this My body, O Gudākesha (Arjuna), and anything else that you like to see.

SRIMAD-BHAGAVAD-GITA

न तु मां शक्यसे द्रष्टु-मनेनैव स्वचक्षुषा ।
दिव्यं ददामि ते चक्षुः पश्य मे योग-मैश्वरम् ॥८॥

सञ्जय उवाच—

एवमुक्त्वा ततो राजन् महा-योगेश्वरो हरिः ।
दर्शयामास पार्थाय परमं रूपमैश्वरम् ॥ ९ ॥

8. But you will not be able to see Me just with these eyes of yours; I am giving unto you the celestial eye, behold My divine miracle.

Sanjaya said:

9. O king, having spoken thus, Hari, the great lord of Yoga, next showed to Pārtha the supreme divine form.

अनेक वक्त्र-नयन-मनेकाद्भुत-दर्शनम् ।
अनेक-दिव्याभरणं दिव्यानेकोद्यतायुधम् ॥ १० ॥
दिव्य-माल्याम्बर-धरं दिव्य-गन्धानुलेपनम् ।
सर्वाश्चर्य-मयं देवं अनन्तं विश्वतो-मुखम् ॥ ११ ॥

10. Having many mouths and eyes, and containing many a wonderful sight, with many heavenly ornaments and wielding many heavenly uplifted weapons.

11. Wearing celestial garlands and apparel, anointed with heavenly perfumes, full of wonders, resplendent, infinite and having faces on every side.

SRIMAD-BHAGAVAD-GITA

दिवि सूर्य-सहस्रस्य भवे-द्युगप-दुत्थिता ।
यदि भाः सदृशी सा स्याद्भास-स्तस्य महात्मनः॥१२॥

तत्रैकस्थं जगत्कृत्स्नं प्रविभक्त-मनेकधा ।
अपश्य-द्देवदेवस्य शरीरे पाण्डव-स्तदा ॥ १३ ॥

12.   If the effulgence of a thousand suns were to appear
in the skies simultaneously, it might compare somewhat with
the splendour of that great form.

13.   Then the son of Pāndu saw the entire universe
with its manifold divisions united there, in the body of the
God of gods.

ततः स विस्मयाविष्टो हृष्ट-रोमा धनञ्जयः ।
प्रणम्य शिरसा देवं कृताञ्जलि-रभाषत ॥ १४ ॥

अर्जुन उवाच—
पश्यामि देवांस्तव देव देहे सर्वांस्तथा भूतविशेष-सङ्घान् ।
ब्रह्माण-मीशं कमलासनस्थ-मृषींश्च सर्वा-नुरगांश्च दिव्यान् ॥

14. Then Dhananjaya, filled with wonder and his hairs standing on end, bowing his head before the Lord said with joined palms.

15. In Your body, O Lord, I see the gods, as also all the hosts of various beings, Brahmā, the ruler seated on his lotus-seat, all the heavenly sages and serpents.

अनेक-बाहूदर-वक्त्र-नेत्रं पश्यामि त्वां सर्वतोऽनन्तरूपम् ।
नान्तं न मध्यं न पुनस्तवादिं पश्यामि विश्वेश्वर विश्वरूप॥१६॥
किरीटिनं गदिनं चक्रिणं च तेजोराशिं सर्वतो दीप्ति-मन्तम् ।
पश्यामि त्वां दुर्निरीक्ष्यं समन्ता-द्दीप्तानलार्क-द्युति-मप्रमेयम् ॥

16. I see You with many hands, bellies, mouths and eyes, possessing infinite forms on every side; O Lord of the universe, O You of universal form, I see, however, neither Your end, nor middle nor Your beginning.

17. I see You all around with the diadem, mace and disc, a mass of light resplendent on all sides, blinding, with the effulgence of the blazing fire and sun, and immeasurable.

त्वमक्षरं परमं वेदितव्यं त्वमस्य विश्वस्य परं निधानम् ।
त्वमव्ययः शाश्वत-धर्म-गोप्ता सनातनस्त्वं पुरुषो मतो मे ॥१८॥
अनादि-मध्यान्त-मनन्त-वीर्य-मनन्त-बाहुं शशि-सूर्य-नेत्रम् ।
पश्यामि त्वां दीप्त-हुताश-वक्त्रं स्वतेजसा विश्वमिदं तपन्तम् ॥

18. You are the imperishable, the Supreme, the thing to be known, You are the supreme resting place of this universe, You are undecaying and the preserver of the eternal religion; I regard You as the primeval Being.

19. I see You as one with no beginning, middle, or end, of infinite prowess, with infinite arms, with the sun and moon for Your eyes and the blazing fire in Your mouths, scorching this universe with Your radiance.

SRIMAD-BHAGAVAD-GITA

द्यावापृथिव्यो-रिदमन्तरं हि व्याप्तं त्वयैकेन दिशश्च सर्वाः ।
दृष्ट्वाद्भुतं रूपमुग्रं तवेदं लोक-त्रयं प्रव्यथितं महात्मन् ॥२०॥

अमी हि त्वां सुरसङ्घा विशन्ति केचि-द्भीताः प्राञ्जलयो गृणन्ति ।
स्वस्तीत्युक्त्वा महर्षि-सिद्ध-सङ्घाः स्तुवन्ति त्वां स्तुतिभिः
पुष्कलाभिः ॥ २१ ॥

20. This space betwixt heaven and earth is pervaded by You only, as also all the quarters ; seeing this wonderful terrible form of Yours, the three worlds are extremely afflicted, O great Soul.

21. Verily, these hosts of gods are entering into You, some being frightened are praising You with joined palms, while the bands of great sages and perfected souls, uttering the word 'peace', are praising You with numerous hymns.

रुद्रादित्या वसवो ये च साध्या विश्वेऽश्विनौ मरुतश्चोष्मपाश्च ।
गन्धर्व-यक्षासुर-सिद्ध-सङ्घा वीक्षन्ते त्वां विस्मिताश्चैव सर्वे ॥२२॥

रूपं महत्ते बहु-वक्त्र-नेत्रं महाबाहो बहु-बाहूरु-पादम् ।
बहूदरं बहु-दंष्ट्राकरालं दृष्ट्वा लोकाः प्रव्यथिता-स्तथाहम् ॥२३॥

22. The Rudras, the Adityas, the Vasus and the Sādhyas, the Vishvadevas, the two Asvins, the Maruts, the manes, the Gandharvas, the Yakshas, the Asuras and, bands of Siddhas—all these are verily looking at You aghast.

23. O mighty-armed one, seeing Your great form consisting of many 'mouths and eyes, many arms, thighs and feet, and many bellies, and fearful with many tusks, the worlds are awe-struck, and so am I.

SRIMAD-BHAGAVAD-GITA

नभःस्पृशं दीप्त-मनेक-वर्णं व्यात्ताननं दीप्त-विशाल-नेत्रम् ।
दृष्ट्वा हि त्वां प्रव्यथितान्तरात्मा धृतिं न विन्दामि शमं
च विष्णो ॥ २४ ॥

दंष्ट्राकरालानि च ते मुखानि दृष्ट्वैव कालानल-सन्निभानि ।
दिशो न जाने न लभे च शर्म प्रसीद देवेश जगन्निवास॥२५॥

24. O Vishnu, seeing You touching the sky, blazing,
of many hues, with gaping mouths and large fiery eyes, I am
frightened at heart, and I feel neither fortitude nor peace.

25. Seeing verily Your mouths fearful with teeth, and
blazing like the fire of dissolution, I know not the cardinal
points, nor do I find pleasure ; O Lord of the gods, O
abode of the universe, be merciful.

अमी च त्वां धृतराष्ट्रस्य पुत्राः सर्वे सहैवावनिपाल-सङ्घैः ।
भीष्मो द्रोणः सूतपुत्र-स्तथासौ सहास्मदीयै-रपि योधमुख्यैः ॥

वक्त्राणि ते त्वरमाणा विशन्ति दंष्ट्राकरालानि भयानकानि ।
केचि-द्विलग्ना दशनान्तरेषु संदृश्यन्ते चूर्णितै-रुत्तमाङ्गैः ॥२७॥

26-27. All those sons of Dhritarāshtra along with hosts of kings, Bhishma, Drona, as also that charioteer's son (Karna) together with the principal warriors on our side are entering in a rush into Your terrible jaws fearful with teeth; some are seen sticking in the interstices of the teeth with their heads smashed.

SRIMAD-BHAGAVAD-GITA

यथा नदीनां बहवोऽम्बु-वेगाः समुद्रमेवाभिमुखा द्रवन्ति ।
तथा तवामी नरलोक-वीरा विशन्ति वक्त्राण्यभिविज्वलन्ति ॥

यथा प्रदीप्तं ज्वलनं पतङ्गा विशन्ति नाशाय समृद्ध-वेगाः ।
तथैव नाशाय विशन्ति लोका-स्तवापि वक्त्राणि समृद्ध-वेगाः ॥

28. As many currents of water from rivers flow towards the sea alone, even so do those heroes in the world of men enter Your mouths, flaming all round.

29. As moths enter a blazing fire with great speed only to be destroyed, even so are these people also entering into Your mouths with great speed just to be destroyed.

THE VISION OF THE UNIVERSAL FORM

लेलिह्यसे ग्रसमानः समन्ताल्लोकान् समग्रान् वदनैर्ज्वलद्भिः ।
तेजोभिरापूर्य जगत्समग्रं भासस्तवोग्राः प्रतपन्ति विष्णो ॥३०
आख्याहि मे को भवानुग्ररूपो नमोऽस्तु ते देववर प्रसीद ।
विज्ञातुमिच्छामि भवन्तमाद्यं न हि प्रजानामि तव प्रवृत्तिम् ॥

30. You are licking all these people on all sides while devouring them with Your flaming mouths; filling the entire world with its radiance, Your fierce glow is scorching it, O Vishnu.

31. Tell me who You are, of ferocious form; salutations to You; O great God, be pleased. I like to know You, the primeval Being; for I do not comprehend Your inclination.

श्रीभगवानुवाच—

कालोऽस्मि लोकक्षयकृत् प्रवृद्धो लोकान् समाहर्तु-मिह प्रवृत्तः ।
ऋतेऽपि त्वां न भविष्यन्ति सर्वे येऽवस्थिताः प्रत्यनीकेषु योधाः ॥

तस्मात् त्वमुत्तिष्ठ यशो लभस्व
जित्वा शत्रून् भुङ्क्ष्व राज्यं समृद्धम् ।
मयैवैते निहताः पूर्वमेव निमित्त-मात्रं भव सव्यसाचिन् ॥३२॥

32. I am the terrible Time, the destroyer of people, and am here proceeding to destroy them ; even without you, all these warriors in every division shall cease to be.

33. Therefore arise and attain fame, and conquering your enemies, enjoy a flourishing kingdom. By Me alone have these been killed already. O Savyasāchin (Arjuna), you be merely an instrument.

THE VISION OF THE UNIVERSAL FORM

द्रोणं च भीष्मं च जयद्रथं च कर्णं तथान्यानपि योधवीरान् ।
मया हतांस्त्वं जहि मा व्यथिष्ठा युध्यस्व जेतासि रणे सपत्नान् ॥

सञ्जय उवाच—

एतच्छ्रुत्वा वचनं केशवस्य कृताञ्जलिर्वेपमानः किरीटी ।
नमस्कृत्वा भूय एवाह कृष्णं सगद्गदं भीतभीतः प्रणम्य ॥ ३५ ॥

34. Kill Drona, Bhishma, Jayadratha, Karna as also other great warriors, already killed by Me; be not distressed. Fight, you will conquer your enemies in battle.

Sanjaya said :

35. Hearing these words of Keshava (Sri Krishna), the trembling Arjuna, saluted with folded palms and said again to Sri Krishna in faltering accents, bowing down and in great fear.

SRIMAD-BHAGAVAD-GITA

अर्जुन उवाच—

स्थाने हृषीकेश तव प्रकीर्त्या जगत् प्रहृष्य-त्यनुरज्यते च ।
रक्षांसि भीतानि दिशो द्रवन्ति सर्वे नमस्यन्ति च सिद्धसङ्घाः ॥
कस्माच्च ते न नमेरन् महात्मन् गरीयसे ब्रह्मणोऽप्यादिकर्त्रे ।
अनन्त देवेश जगन्निवास त्वमक्षरं सदस-त्तत्परं यत् ॥ ३७ ॥

Arjuna said :

36. It is mete, O Hrishikesa (Krishna) that by Your glorification the world gets delighted and attracted (towards You), the demons, getting frightened, run in all directions, and all the hosts of perfected beings bow down to You.

37. And why should they not, O noble soul, salute You the original Agent, who are greater than even Brahmā? O infinite being, O ruler of the gods, O abode of the world, You are the imperishable, the manifest and the unmanifest, and that which is beyond both.

त्वमादिदेवः पुरुषः पुराण-स्त्वमस्य विश्वस्य परं निधानम् ।
वेत्तासि वेद्यं च परं च धाम त्वया ततं विश्व-मनन्तरूप ॥ ३८ ॥

वायु-र्यमोऽग्नि-र्वरुणः शशाङ्कः प्रजापतिस्त्वं प्रपितामहश्च ।
नमो नमस्तेऽस्तु सहस्रकृत्वः पुनश्च भूयोऽपि नमो नमस्ते ॥३९

38. You are the primeval God, the ancient Being, You are the supreme repository of this universe, You are the knower and the knowable, and the highest abode; O You of infinite form, by You is the universe pervaded.

39. You are the Wind-god, Death, Fire, the Sea-gods, the moon, Prajāpati (Brahmā) and also the great-grandsire;

SRIMAD-BHAGAVAD-GITA

नमः पुरस्ता-द्थ पृष्ठतस्ते नमोऽस्तु ते सर्वत एव सर्व ।

अनन्तवीर्यामित-विक्रमस्त्वं सर्वं समाप्नोषि ततोऽसि सर्वः ॥४०

salutations, a thousandfold salutation to You salutation again and again to You, salutations.

40. O All, salutations to You in front and from behind, salutations to You all round; You are of infinite prowess, of immeasurable valour; You pervade everything, and so You are everything.

सखेति मत्वा प्रसभं यदुक्तं हे कृष्ण हे यादव हे सखेति ।
अजानता महिमानं तवेदं मया प्रमादात्प्रणयेन वापि ॥ ४१ ॥
यच्चावहासार्थ-मसत्कृतोऽसि विहार-शय्यासन-भोजनेषु ।
एकोऽथवाप्यच्युत तत्समक्षं तत्क्षामये त्वामहमप्रमेयम् ॥ ४२ ॥

41-42. Whatever I, not knowing the greatness and this form of Yours, may have said to You importunately, out of ignorance or affection, addressing You as, O Krishna, O Yādava, O friend, regarding You as my friend, and in whatever way you may have been slighted out of fun at sport, in bed, on the seat, or in eating, either alone or in company—all that, O Achyuta, I entreat You, the incomprehensible one, to forgive.

पितासि लोकस्य चराचरस्य त्वमस्य पूज्यश्च गुरु-गरीयान् ।
न त्वत्समोऽस्त्यभ्यधिकः कुतोऽन्यो लोकत्रयेऽप्यप्रतिम-प्रभाव॥
तस्मात् प्रणम्य प्रणिधाय कायं प्रसादये त्वा-महमीश-मीड्यम् ।
पितेव पुत्रस्य सखेव सख्युः प्रियः प्रियायार्हसि देव सोढुम् ॥

43. You are the father of this world of moving and unmoving things, adorable and the teacher, greater than any superior, there is none indeed equal to You in all the three worlds, how then could there be one greater than You, O You of unrivalled power?

44. Therefore prostrating the body and bowing down to You, I entreat You, the adorable Lord, to be gracious; just as a father forgives his son, a friend his friend, and a lover his beloved one (to please her), even so You should forgive me, O Lord.

अदृष्टपूर्वं हृषितोऽस्मि दृष्ट्वा भयेन च प्रव्यथितं मनो मे।
तदेव मे दर्शय देव रूपं प्रसीद देवेश जगन्निवास॥ ४५॥
किरीटिनं गदिनं चक्र-हस्त-मिच्छामि त्वां द्रष्टुमहं तथैव।
तेनैव रूपेण चतुर्भुजेन सहस्रबाहो भव विश्वमूर्ते॥ ४६॥

45. O Lord, seeing what has never been seen before, I am overjoyed, but my mind is extremely agitated through fear; show me that very (old) form; O God of gods, O abode of the universe, be gracious.

46. I like to see You as before diademed, bearing a mace and disc in Your hands; assume that very form with four arms, O thousand-armed one, O You of universal form.

SRIMAD-BHAGAVAD-GITA

श्री भगवानुवाच—

मया प्रसन्नेन तवार्जुनेदं रूपं परं दर्शित-मात्मयोगात् ।
तेजोमयं विश्व-मनन्त-माद्यं यन्मे त्वदन्येन न दृष्टपूर्वम् ॥ ४७ ॥

न वेद-यज्ञाध्ययनै-र्न दानै-र्न च क्रियाभि-र्न तपोभिरुग्रैः ।
एवंरूपः शक्य अहं नृलोके द्रष्टुं त्वदन्येन कुरुप्रवीर ॥ ४८ ॥

The Blessed Lord said :

47. Being pleased, I have shown you, O Arjuna, through My Yoga power, this supreme form of Mine, resplendent, universal, infinite and primeval, which has not been seen before by any one else than you.

48. Neither by a study of the Vedas and sacrifices, nor by charity, nor by ceremonies, nor by austere penances, can I be seen in this form, in the world of mortals, by any other person than you, O great hero among the Kurus.

THE VISION OF THE UNIVERSAL FORM

मा ते व्यथा मा च विमूढ-भावो दृष्ट्वा रूपं घोरमीदृङ्ममेदम् ।
व्यपेतभीः प्रीतमनाः पुनस्त्वं तदेव मे रूपमिदं प्रपश्य ॥ ४९ ॥

सञ्जय उवाच—

इत्यर्जुनं वासुदेव-स्तथोक्त्वा स्वकं रूपं दर्शयामास भूयः ।
आश्वासयामास च भीतमेनं भूत्वा पुनः सौम्यवपु-र्महात्मा ॥५०॥

49. Be not agitated, or deluded, seeing this terrible form of Mine; free from fear, and with cheerful mind, see again that very form of Mine.

Sanjaya said:

50. Speaking thus to Arjuna, Vāsudeva (Krishna) again showed His own form; the great soul again cheered up the frightened (Arjuna), assuming His benign body.

SRIMAD-BHAGAVAD-GITA

अर्जुन उवाच—

दृष्ट्वेदं मानुषं रूपं तव सौम्यं जनार्दन ।
इदानीमस्मि संवृत्तः सचेताःप्रकृतिं गतः ॥ ५१ ॥

श्री भगवानुवाच—

सुदुर्दर्शमिदं रूपं दृष्टवानसि यन्मम ।
देवा अप्यस्य रूपस्य नित्यं दर्शन-काङ्क्षिणः ॥ ५२ ॥

Arjuna said :

51. O Janārdana, seeing this benign human form of Yours I have now become self-composed and come to normal state.

The Blessed Lord said :

52. Exceedingly difficult is it to see this form of Mine that you have seen; even the gods are ever eager to see this form.

नाहं वेदैर्न तपसा न दानेन न चेज्यया ।
शक्य एवंविधो द्रष्टुं दृष्टवानसि मां यथा ॥ ५३ ॥

भक्त्या त्वनन्यया शक्य अहमेवंविधोऽर्जुन ।
ज्ञातुं द्रष्टुं च तत्त्वेन प्रवेष्टुं च परंतप ॥ ५४ ॥

53. Neither by the Vedas, nor by austerities, nor by gifts, nor by sacrifices, am I visible in this form, as you have seen Me.

54. But by undivided devotion, O Arjuna, can I in this form be known and realized in truth and entered into, O scorcher of foes.

मत्कर्मकृन्मत्परमो मद्भक्तः सङ्गवर्जितः ।
निर्वैरः सर्वभूतेषु यः स मामेति पाण्डव ॥ ५५ ॥

इति श्रीमद्भगवद्गीतासूपनिषत्सु ब्रह्मविद्यायां योगशास्त्रे
श्रीकृष्णार्जुनसंवादे विश्वरूपदर्शनयोगो नाम
एकादशोऽध्यायः ॥

55. He who works for Me, has Me for the supreme goal, is devoted to Me, and non-attached, and bears no hatred towards any creature, he attains to Me, O Pāndava.

॥ द्वादशोऽध्यायः ॥
(भक्तियोगः)

अर्जुन उवाच—
एवं सतत-युक्ता ये भक्तास्त्वां पर्युपासते ।
ये चाप्यक्षर-मव्यक्तं तेषां के योगवित्तमाः ॥ १ ॥

CHAPTER XII
THE WAY OF DEVOTION

Arjuna said:

1. Between those devotees who worship You, being thus ever devoted, and those who worship the Imperishable, the Unmanifest, who are better versed in Yoga?

श्री भगवानुवाच—

मय्यावेश्य मनो ये मां नित्ययुक्ता उपासते ।
श्रद्धया परयोपेतास्ते मे युक्ततमा मताः ॥ २ ॥

ये त्वक्षर-मनिर्देश्य-मव्यक्तं पर्युपासते ।
सर्वत्रग-मचिन्त्यं च कूटस्थ-मचलं ध्रुवम् ॥ ३ ॥

The Blessed Lord said :

2. Those who worship Me fixing their mind on Me,
ever devoted, and endowed with supreme faith—them I
regard as the best Yogins.

3-4 but they who worship the Imperishable, Indescri-
bable, Unmanifest, All-pervading, Inconceivable, Changeless,

सन्नियम्येन्द्रियग्रामं सर्वत्र समबुद्धयः ।
ते प्राप्नुवन्ति मामेव सर्वभूतहिते रताः ॥ ४ ॥

क्लेशोऽधिकतरस्तेषा-मव्यक्तासक्त-चेतसाम् ।
अव्यक्ता हि गतिर्दुःखं देहवद्भिः-रवाप्यते ॥ ५ ॥

Immovable and Eternal, controlling well their senses, even-minded everywhere and devoted to the good of all beings, (also) attain Me alone.

5. The trouble of those whose minds are attached to the unmanifest is greater; for the way of the Unmanifest is attained with difficulty by the embodied soul.

SRIMAD-BHAGAVAD-GITA

ये तु सर्वाणि कर्माणि मयि सन्न्यस्य मत्पराः ।
अनन्येनैव योगेन मां ध्यायन्त उपासते ॥ ६ ॥

तेषामहं समुद्धर्ता मृत्यु-संसार-सागरात् ।
भवामि नचिरात् पार्थ मय्यावेशित-चेतसाम् ॥ ७ ॥

6-7. Those, however, who renouncing all actions in
Me, and being attached to Me, worship Me with unswerving
devotion through meditation—these people, who have fixed
their mind on Me, I quickly redeem from this ocean of
transmigratory existence beset with death.

मय्येव मन आधत्स्व मयि बुद्धिं निवेशय ।
निवसिष्यसि मय्येव अत ऊर्ध्वं न संशयः ॥८॥

अथ चित्तं समाधातुं न शक्नोषि मयि स्थिरम् ।
अभ्यास-योगेन ततो मामिच्छाप्तुं धनञ्जय ॥९॥

8. Fix your mind on Me alone, let your intellect rest in Me, you will live in Me alone hereafter; there is no doubt (about it).

9. If, however, you are not able to fix the mind steadily on Me, then through the Yoga of practice seek to attain Me, O Dhananjaya.

SRIMAD-BHAGAVAD-GITA

अभ्यासेऽप्यसमर्थोऽसि मत्कर्म-परमो भव ।
मदर्थमपि कर्माणि कुर्वन् सिद्धिमवाप्स्यसि ॥ १० ॥

अथैत-दप्यशक्तोऽसि कर्तुं मद्योग-माश्रितः ।
सर्वकर्म-फल-त्यागं ततः कुरु यतात्मवान् ॥ ११ ॥

10. If you are unable even to practise, then be solely devoted to rites for Me ; even by doing rites for My sake, you will attain perfection.

11. If, however, you are unable to do even this, then taking refuge in Me and being self-controlled, renounce the fruit of all actions.

श्रेयो हि ज्ञानमभ्यासा-ज्ज्ञानाद्ध्यानं विशिष्यते ।
ध्यानात् कर्मफलत्याग-स्त्यागा-च्छान्ति-रनन्तरम् ॥ १२ ॥
अद्वेष्टा सर्वभूतानां मैत्रः करुण एव च ।
निर्ममो निरहङ्कारः सम-दुःखसुखः क्षमी ॥ १३ ॥
संतुष्टः सततं योगी यतात्मा दृढनिश्चयः ।
मय्यर्पित-मनो-बुद्धिर्यो मद्भक्तः स मे प्रियः ॥ १४ ॥

12. Knowledge is superior to (mere) practice, meditation is superior to knowledge, superior to meditation is renunciation of the fruit of action, from renunciation results peace immediately.

13-14. Non-envious, friendly, and compassionate towards all beings, free from ideas of possession and ego-

SRIMAD-BHAGAVAD-GITA

यस्मा-न्नोद्विजते लोको लोका-न्नोद्विजते च यः ।
हर्षामर्ष-भयोद्वेगै-र्मुक्तो यः स च मे प्रियः ॥ १५ ॥

अनपेक्षः शुचि-र्दक्ष उदासीनो गतव्यथः ।
सर्वारम्भ-परित्यागी यो मद्भक्तः स मे प्रियः ॥ १६ ॥

consciousness, sympathetic in pain and pleasure, forgiving, always contented, contemplative, self-controlled, of firm conviction with his mind and intellect dedicated to Me— such a devotee of Mine is dear to Me.

15. From whom the world gets no trouble, and who gets no trouble from the world, who is free from elation, jealousy, fear and anxiety—he is dear to Me.

16. Independent, clean, dexterous, indifferent, untroubled, and discarding all endeavours—such a devotee of Mine is dear to Me.

यो न हृष्यति न द्वेष्टि न शोचति न काङ्क्षति ।
शुभाशुभ-परित्यागी भक्तिमान् यः स मे प्रियः ॥१७॥
समः शत्रौ च मित्रे च तथा मानापमानयोः ।
शीतोष्ण-सुखदुःखेषु समः सङ्ग-विवर्जितः ॥१८॥
तुल्य-निन्दा-स्तुति-मौनी संतुष्टो येन केनचित् ।
अनिकेतः स्थिरमति-भक्तिमान् मे प्रियो नरः ॥१९॥

17. He who neither rejoices nor dislikes nor grieves nor desires, who renounces good and evil, and who is devoted, is dear to Me.

18-19. Alike to foe and friend, in honour and dishonour, in heat and cold, happiness and misery, free from

ये तु धर्म्यामृत-मिदं यथोक्तं पर्युपासते ।
श्रद्दधाना मत्परमा भक्तास्तेऽतीव मे प्रियाः ॥ २० ॥

इति श्रीमद्भगवद्गीतासूपनिषत्सु ब्रह्मविद्यायां योगशास्त्रे
श्रीकृष्णार्जुनसंवादे भक्तियोगो नाम
द्वादशोऽध्यायः ॥

attachment, alike in praise and censure, reticent, satisfied with anything, without a home, steady in mind—such a devoted person is dear to Me.

20. Those devotees who practise this nectar-like religion just taught with faith, and with Me as their supreme goal, are extremely dear to Me.

———

॥ त्रयोदशोऽध्यायः ॥
(क्षेत्रक्षेत्रज्ञविभागयोगः)

CHAPTER XIII
DISCRIMINATION BETWEEN NATURE AND SOUL

श्री भगवानुवाच—

इदं शरीरं कौन्तेय क्षेत्र-मित्यभिधीयते ।
एतद्यो वेत्ति तं प्राहुः क्षेत्रज्ञ इति तद्विदः ॥ १ ॥

The Blessed Lord Said :

1. This body, O son of Kunti, is called the kshetra, and that which is conscious of it is called Kshetrajna (embodied seif) by those who have knowledge thereof.

SRIMAD-BHAGAVAD-GITA

क्षेत्रज्ञं चापि मां विद्धि सर्वक्षेत्रेषु भारत ।
क्षेत्र-क्षेत्रज्ञयो-र्ज्ञानं यत्तज्ज्ञानं मतं मम ॥ २ ॥
तत्क्षेत्रं यच्च यादृक्च यद्विकारि यतश्च यत् ।
स च यो यत्प्रभावश्च तत्समासेन मे शृणु ॥ ३ ॥ ॥

2. And know the Kshetrajna (embodied self) in all the bodies (Kshetras) to be Myself, O descendant of Bharata. The knowledge of the Kshetra and Kshetrajna (i.e., matter and spirit) is, in My opinion, true knowledge.

3. What that Kshetra is, what it is like, what its modifications are, whence it arises, and what its forms are; and also what the other entity (the Kshetrajna) is, and what its powers are—hear that from Me in brief.

DISCRIMINATION BETWEEN NATURE AND SOUL

ऋषिभि-र्बहुधा गीतं छन्दोभि-र्विविधैः पृथक् ।
ब्रह्मसूत्र-पदैश्चैव हेतुमद्भि-र्विनिश्चितैः ॥ ४ ॥
महाभूता-न्यहङ्कारो बुद्धि-रव्यक्त-मेव च ।
इन्द्रियाणि दशैकं च पञ्च चेन्द्रिय-गोचराः ॥ ५ ॥
इच्छा द्वेषः सुखं दुःखं सङ्घातश्चेतना धृतिः ।
एतत् क्षेत्रं समासेन सविकार-मुदाहृतम् ॥ ६ ॥

4. It has been sung differently by the sages (Rishis) and variously in different Vedic hymns, as also in passages indicative and descriptive of Brahman, furnished with reasons and decisive.

5-6. The (five) great elements, egoism (Ahankara), the intellect, and the unmanifest, the ten sense-organs and the

SRIMAD-BHAGAVAD-GITA

अमानित्व-मदम्भित्व-महिंसा क्षान्ति-राजवम् ।
आचार्योपासनं शौचं स्थैर्य-मात्म-विनिग्रहः ॥ ७ ॥

इन्द्रियार्थेषु वैराग्य-मनहङ्कार एव च ।
जन्म-मृत्यु-जरा-व्याधि-दुःख-दोषानुदर्शनम् ॥ ८ ॥

असक्ति-रनभिष्वङ्गः पुत्र-दार-गृहादिषु ।
नित्यं च समचित्तत्व-मिष्टानिष्टोपपत्तिषु ॥ ९ ॥

one (mind) and the five objects of the senses; desire.
aversion, happiness, misery, the body, intelligence and
patience—thus the Kshetra has been described in brief
together with its modifications.

7-11. Humility, unostentatiousness, harmlessness,
forbearance, uprightness, service to the Guru, purity,

मयि चानन्ययोगेन भक्ति-रव्यभिचारिणी ।
विविक्तदेश-सेवित्व-मरति-र्जनसंसदि ॥ १० ॥

अध्यात्म-ज्ञाननित्यत्वं तत्त्वज्ञानार्थ-दर्शनम् ।
एतज्ज्ञानमिति प्रोक्त-मज्ञानं यदतोऽन्यथा ॥ ११ ॥

steadiness, selfcontrol, dispassion for sense-objects and absence of egoism, seeing misery and evil in birth, death, old age and sickness, nonattachment and non-identification with son, wife, home, etc., always being even-minded whether good or evil befalls, unswerving devotion to Me through the Yoga of nonseparation, resorting to solitude, and aversion for company, always being devoted to spiritual knowledge, perception of the aim of the knowledge of Truth all this is called knowledge. What is different from this is ignorance.

SRIMAD-BHAGAVAD-GITA

ज्ञेयं यत्तत् प्रवक्ष्यामि यज्ज्ञात्वामृत-मश्नुते ।
अनादिमत् परं ब्रह्म न सत्त-न्नासदुच्यते ॥ १२ ॥
सर्वतः पाणिपादं तत् सर्वतोऽक्षिशिरो-मुखम् ।
सर्वतः श्रुतिम-ल्लोके सर्व-मावृत्य तिष्ठति ॥ १३ ॥

12. I shall tell you that which has to be known, knowing which one attains immortality; it is the beginningless, supreme Brahman, which is said to be neither being nor non-being.

13. With hands and feet everywhere, with eyes, heads and faces everywhere, with ears everywhere, It rests pervading everything in this world.

सर्वेन्द्रिय-गुणाभासं सर्वेन्द्रिय-विवर्जितम् ।
असक्तं सर्वभृच्चैव निर्गुणं गुणभोक्तृ च ॥ १४ ॥
बहिरन्तश्च भूताना-मचरं चरमेव च ।
सूक्ष्मत्वा-त्तदविज्ञेयं दूरस्थं चान्तिके च तत् ॥ १५ ॥

14. It is manifest in the functions of the various sense-organs, yet bereft of all sense-organs, unattached, yet sustaining everything, without attributes, yet the protector of the qualities.

15. It is without and within all beings, It is moving and unmoving, being subtle, It is incomprehensible, It is far, yet near.

SRIMAD-BHAGAVAD-GITA

अविभक्तं च भूतेषु विभक्त-मिव च स्थितम् ।
भूतभर्तृ च तज्ज्ञेयं ग्रसिष्णु प्रभविष्णु च ॥ १६ ॥
ज्योतिषामपि तज्ज्योति-स्तमसः पर-मुच्यते ।
ज्ञानं ज्ञेयं ज्ञानगम्यं हृदि सर्वस्य विष्ठितम् ॥ १७ ॥

16. It is undivided in beings and yet remains as if divided; that Knowable is the sustainer of beings as also the destroyer and creator.

17. It is the Light of lights and is said to be beyond all darkness, It is knowledge, the knowable and accessible through knowledge, and is implanted in the heart of all beings.

इति क्षेत्रं तथा ज्ञानं ज्ञेयं चोक्तं समासतः ।
मद्भक्त एतद्विज्ञाय मद्भावायोपपद्यते ॥ १८ ॥

प्रकृतिं पुरुषं चैव विद्ध्यनादी उभावपि ।
विकारांश्च गुणांश्चैव विद्धि प्रकृति-संभवान् ॥ १९ ॥

18. Thus the Kshetra, knowledge and the Knowable have been stated in brief. Knowing this, My devotee becomes fit to attain My being.

19. Know both Prakriti and Purusha to be beginningless and know the evolutes and the Gunas as born of Prakriti (Nature).

SRIMAD-BHAGAVAD-GITA

कार्य-कारण-कर्तृत्वे हेतुः प्रकृति-रुच्यते ।
पुरुषः सुखदुःखानां भोक्तृत्वे हेतुरुच्यते ॥ २० ॥
पुरुषः प्रकृतिस्थो हि भुङ्क्ते प्रकृतिजान्-गुणान् ।
कारणं गुणसङ्गोऽस्य सदसद्योनि-जन्मसु ॥ २१ ॥

20. With respect to the production of the effect (body) and the causes (the senses), Prakriti is said to be the cause, while with respect to the experience of happiness and misery, the Purusha is said to be the cause.

21. For the Purusha residing in Prakriti experiences the Gunas born of Prakriti. The cause of its birth from good and evil sources is its attachment to the Gunas (senses).

उपद्रष्टानुमन्ता च भर्ता भोक्ता महेश्वरः ।
परमात्मेति चाप्युक्तो देहेऽस्मिन् पुरुषः परः ॥ २२ ॥

य एवं वेत्ति पुरुषं प्रकृतिं च गुणैः सह ।
सर्वथा वर्तमानोऽपि न स भूयोऽभिजायते ॥ २३ ॥

22. The supreme Purusha in this body is called the Onlooker, the Permitter, the Nourisher, the Protector, the great Lord, and also the supreme Self.

23. He who thus knows the Purusha and the Prakriti together with the Gunas is not born again, whatever his mode of life.

SRIMAD-BHAGAVAD-GITA

ध्यानेनात्मनि पश्यन्ति केचि-दात्मान-मात्मना ।
अन्ये सांख्येन योगेन कर्मयोगेन चापरे ॥ २४ ॥

अन्ये त्वेव-मजानन्तः श्रुत्वान्येभ्य उपासते ।
तेऽपि चातितरन्त्येव मृत्युं श्रुति-परायणाः ॥ २५ ॥

24. Some see the Self in the Self by the self through meditation, others by (the path of) knowledge, some others by Yoga and (still) others by the path of action.

25. Others (again), not knowing thus, worship by hearing from others; verily, they also, being devoted to hearing, go beyond death.

यावत् संजायते किञ्चित् सत्त्वं स्थावर-जङ्गमम् ।
क्षेत्र-क्षेत्रज्ञ-संयोगा-त्तद्विद्धि भरतर्षभ ॥ २६ ॥

समं सर्वेषु भूतेषु तिष्ठन्तं परमेश्वरम् ।
विनश्यत्स्वविनश्यन्तं यः पश्यति स पश्यति ॥ २७ ॥

26. Whatever being is born, moving or unmoving (animate or inanimate), know that, O best of Bharatas, to come from the mixing of the Kshetra and the Kshetrajna.

27. He who sees the supreme Lord abiding equally in all beings, the imperishable amidst the perishable—he sees indeed.

SRIMAD-BHAGAVAD-GITA

समं पश्यन्हि सर्वत्र समवस्थित-मीश्वरम् ।
न हिनस्त्यात्मनात्मानं ततो याति परां गतिम् ॥ २८ ॥

प्रकृत्यैव च कर्माणि क्रियमाणानि सर्वशः ।
यः पश्यति तथात्मान-मकर्तारं स पश्यति ॥ २९ ॥

28. For seeing the Lord abiding equally everywhere, he does not injure the Self by the self; therefore he attains the supreme goal.

29. He who sees that actions are in every way performed only by Prakriti, and likewise (sees) the Self as the non-doer, (alone) sees (in truth).

यदा भूत-पृथग्भाव-मेकस्थ-मनुपश्यति ।
तत एव च विस्तारं ब्रह्म संपद्यते तदा ॥ ३० ॥

अनादित्वा-न्निर्गुणत्वात् परमात्माय-मव्ययः ।
शरीरस्थोऽपि कौन्तेय न करोति न लिप्यते ॥ ३१ ॥

30. When one sees the diversity of beings as abiding in the one (Prakriti) and their emanation from that one alone, then one becomes Brahman.

31. This supreme Self, being without a beginning and devoid of attributes, is immutable. Though residing in the body, O son of Kunti, It neither acts nor is It attached.

SRIMAD-BHAGAVAD-GITA

यथा सर्वगतं सौक्ष्म्या-दाकाशं नोपलिप्यते ।
सर्वत्रावस्थितो देहे तथात्मा नोपलिप्यते ॥ ३२ ॥

यथा प्रकाशयत्येकः कृत्स्नं लोक-मिमं रविः ।
क्षेत्रं क्षेत्री तथा कृत्स्नं प्रकाशयति भारत ॥ ३३ ॥

32. Just as the all-pervading ether, being subtle, is not contaminated, so is the Self located in every body not contaminated.

33. Even as the one sun illumines the whole world even so, O descendant of Bharata, does the embodied soul illumine all bodies.

क्षेत्र-क्षेत्रज्ञयोरेवमन्तरं ज्ञान-चक्षुषा ।
भूत-प्रकृति-मोक्षं च ये विदुर्यान्ति ते परम् ॥ ३४ ॥

इति श्रीमद्भगवद्गीतासूपनिषत्सु ब्रह्मविद्यायां योगशास्त्रे
श्रीकृष्णार्जुनसंवादे क्षेत्रक्षेत्रज्ञविभागयोगो नाम
त्रयोदशोऽध्यायः ॥

34. Those who thus perceive with the eye of knowledge the difference between the Kshetra and the Kshetrajna as also (the means of) freedom from the cause of beings (Nature)—attain the Supreme.

॥ चतुर्दशोऽध्यायः ॥
(गुणत्रयविभागयोगः)

श्री भगवानुवाच—

परं भूयः प्रवक्ष्यामि ज्ञानानां ज्ञान-मुत्तमम् ।
यज्ज्ञात्वा मुनयः सर्वे परां सिद्धि-मितो गताः ॥१॥

CHAPTER XIV
THE SEPARATION OF THE THREE GUNAS

The Blessed Lord said :

1, I shall tell you again the supreme knowledge—the best of all knowledges, knowing which all the sages have attained supreme felicity from hence.

इदं ज्ञान-मुपाश्रित्य मम साधर्म्य-मागताः ।
सर्गेऽपि नोपजायन्ते प्रलये न व्यथन्ति च ॥ २ ॥

मम योनि-र्महद्ब्रह्म तस्मिन् गर्भं दधाम्यहम् ।
संभवः सर्वभूतानां ततो भवति भारत ॥ ३ ॥

2. By resorting to this knowledge they, having attained to My nature, are not reborn even at the time of creation nor are they distressed at the time of dissolution.

3. The great Nature is My womb; in that I place the germ, and from that, O descendant of Bharata, is the origin of all beings.

SRIMAD-BHAGAVAD-GITA

सर्वयोनिषु कौन्तेय मूर्तयः संभवन्ति याः ।
तासां ब्रह्म महद्योनिरहं बीज-प्रदः पिता ॥ ४ ॥

सत्त्वं रजस्तम इति गुणाः प्रकृति-संभवाः ।
निबध्नन्ति महाबाहो देहे देहिन-मव्ययम् ॥ ५ ॥

4. Whatever forms, O son of Kunti, are born in different wombs, of them the great Nature is the womb, and I am the seed-giving father.

5. Sattva, Rajas and Tamas—these Gunas, O mighty-armed one, that are born of Nature (Prakritj), bind fast the immutable, embodied being in this body.

तत्र सत्त्वं निर्मलत्वात् प्रकाशकमनामयम् ।
सुखसङ्गेन बध्नाति ज्ञान-सङ्गेन चानघ ॥ ६ ॥

रजो रागात्मकं विद्धि तृष्णा-सङ्ग-समुद्भवम् ।
तन्निबध्नाति कौन्तेय कर्मसङ्गेन देहिनम् ॥ ७ ॥

6. Of these, Sattva on account of its stainlessness is luminous and free from evil; it binds (the embodied self) by attachment to happiness and by attachment to knowledge, O sinless one (Arjuna).

7. Know Rajas to be of the nature of passion, the source of desire and attachment: O son of Kunti, it binds fast the embodied self by attachment to action.

SRIMAD-BHAGAVAD-GITA

तमस्त्वज्ञानजं विद्धि मोहनं सर्वदेहिनाम् ।
प्रमादालस्य-निद्राभि-स्तन्निबध्नाति भारत ॥ ८ ॥

सत्त्वं सुखे सञ्जयति रजः कर्मणि भारत ।
ज्ञान-माव्तय तु तमः प्रमादे सञ्जयत्युत ॥ ९ ॥

8. But know Tamas to be born of ignorance and deluding all embodied beings : it binds fast, O descendant of Bharata, through inadvertence, laziness and sleep.

9. Sattva binds (one) to happiness, Rajas, O descendant of Bharata, (binds one) to work, while Tamas by covering knowledge binds (one) to inadvertence, etc.

रजस्तमश्चाभिभूय सत्त्वं भवति भारत ।
रजः सत्त्वं तमश्चैव तमः सत्त्वं रजस्तथा ॥ १० ॥
सर्वद्वारेषु देहेऽस्मिन् प्रकाश उपजायते ।
ज्ञानं यदा तदा विद्या-द्विवृद्धं सत्त्वमित्युत ॥ ११ ॥

10. Sattva manifests, O descendant of Bharata, overpowering Rajas and Tamas; Rajas (manifests) overpowering Sattva and Tamas and likewise Tamas (manifests) overpowering Sattva and Rajas.

11. When through all the sense-openings in this body the light of knowledge radiates, then indeed one should know that Sattva predominates.

SRIMAD-BHAGAVAD-GITA

लोभः प्रवृत्ति-रारम्भः कर्मणा-मशमः स्पृहा ।
रजस्येतानि जायन्ते विवृद्धे भरतर्षभ ॥ १२ ॥

अप्रकाशोऽप्रवृत्तिश्च प्रमादो मोह एव च ।
तमस्येतानि जायन्ते विवृद्धे कुरुनन्दन ॥ १३॥

12. Greed, activity, undertaking of works, restlessness, desire—these prevail, O best of the Bharatas, when Rajas predominates.

13. Darkness, inactivity, inadvertence, as also delusion—these prevail, O descendant of Kuru (Arjuna), when Tamas predominates.

यदा सत्त्वे प्रवृद्धे तु प्रलयं याति देहभृत् ।
तदोत्तमविदां लोका-नमलान् प्रतिपद्यते ॥ १४ ॥

रजसि प्रलयं गत्वा कर्मसङ्गिषु जायते ।
तथा प्रलीन-स्तमसि मूढ-योनिषु जायते ॥ १५ ॥

14. If the embodied self meets with death when Sattva is predominant, then it attains the pure spheres of the worshippers of the highest deities.

15. If it meets with death when Rajas is predominant, then it is born amongst those who are attached to work; likewise if it meets with death when Tamas is predominant, then it is born in the wombs of irrational species.

SRIMAD-BHAGAVAD-GITA

कर्मणः सुकृतस्याहुः सात्त्विकं निर्मलं फलम् ।
रजसस्तु फलं दुःख-मज्ञानं तमसः फलम् ॥ १६ ॥

सत्त्वात् सञ्जायते ज्ञानं रजसो लोभ एव च ।
प्रमाद मोहौ तमसो भवतोऽज्ञानमेव च ॥ १७ ॥

16.   The result of virtuous action is said to be Sāttvika
and pure, the result of Rajas is pain, while ignorance is the
result of Tamas.

17.   From Sattva results knowledge, from Rajas only
greed, and from Tamas nothing but inadvertence, delusion
and ignorance.

ऊर्ध्वं गच्छन्ति सत्त्वस्था मध्ये तिष्ठन्ति राजसाः ।
जघन्य-गुण-वृत्तिस्था अधो गच्छन्ति तामसाः ॥१८॥

नान्यं गुणेभ्यः कर्तारं यदा द्रष्टानुपश्यति ।
गुणेभ्यश्च परं वेत्ति मद्भावं सोऽधिगच्छति ॥१९॥

18. Those who abide in Sattva go upwards (to higher spheres), the Rājasika dwell in the middle (spheres), and the Tāmasika, dwelling in the functions of the lowest Guna, go downwards (to lower spheres).

19. When the seer beholds no (active) agent other than Gunas, and knows that which is beyond the Gunas, he attains My being.

गुणानेतानतीत्य त्रीन् देही देहसमुद्भवान् ।
जन्म-मृत्यु-जरादुःखै-र्विमुक्तोऽमृतमश्नुते ॥ २० ॥

अर्जुन उवाच—
कैर्लिङ्गै-स्त्रीन्गुणा-नेता-नतीतो भवति प्रभो ।
किमाचारः कथं चैतांस्त्रीन् गुणा-नतिवर्तते ॥ २१ ॥

20. Having transcended these three Gunas, which are
the cause of this body, the embodied self, bereft of birth,
death, old age and misery, attains immortality.

Arjuna said :

21. By what characteristics, O Lord, is one who has
transcended these three Gunas known? What is his conduct,
and how does he transcend these three Gunas?

श्री भगवानुवाच—

प्रकाशं च प्रवृत्तिं च मोहमेव च पाण्डव ।
न द्वेष्टि संप्रवृत्तानि न निवृत्तानि काङ्क्षति ॥२२॥
उदासीनव-दासीनो गुणैर्यो न विचाल्यते ।
गुणा वर्तन्त इत्येव योऽवतिष्ठति नेङ्गते ॥ २३ ॥

The Blessed Lord said:

22. He who does not hate when the light (of knowledge), activity and delusion arise, O son of Pāndu, nor desires them when they cease;

23. He who rests like one indifferent and is not disturbed by the Gunas, who, realizing that the Gunas alone function, is steady and does not waver;

SRIMAD-BHAGAVAD-GITA

समदुःखसुखः स्वस्थः सम-लोष्टाश्म-काञ्चनः ।
तुल्यप्रियाप्रियो धीर-स्तुल्यनिन्दात्म-संस्तुतिः ॥२४॥
मानापमानयो-स्तुल्य-स्तुल्यो मित्रारिपक्षयोः ।
सर्वारम्भ-परित्यागी गुणातीतः स उच्यते ॥ २५ ॥

24. Alike in pleasure and pain, Self-abiding, regarding a clod of earth, a stone and gold as of equal worth, the same towards agreeable and disagreeable objects, calm, and the same to praise and blame bestowed on him;

25. The same in honour and dishonour, the same towards friend and foe, habituated to renounce all actions—such a person is said to have transcended the Gunas.

मां च योऽव्यभिचारेण भक्तियोगेन सेवते ।
स गुणान् समतीत्यैतान् ब्रह्मभूयाय कल्पते ॥ २६ ॥
ब्रह्मणो हि प्रतिष्ठाह-ममृतस्याव्ययस्य च ।
शाश्वतस्य च धर्मस्य सुखस्यैकान्तिकस्य च ॥२७॥

इति श्रीमद्भगवद्गीतासूपनिषत्सु ब्रह्मविद्यायां योगशास्त्रे
श्रीकृष्णार्जुनसंवादे गुणत्रयविभागयोगो नाम
चतुर्दशोऽध्यायः ॥

26. He who serves Me alone through the unswerving Yoga of devotion, transcends these Gunas and becomes fit for the state of Brahman.

27. For I am the embodiment of Brahman, of immutable immortality, of the eternal religion and of absolute bliss.

॥ पञ्चदशोऽध्यायः ॥
(पुरुषोत्तमयोगः)

श्री भगवानुवाच—

ऊर्ध्व-मूल-मधःशाख-मश्वत्थं प्राहु-रव्ययम् ।
छन्दांसि यस्य पर्णानि यस्तं वेद स वेदवित् ॥१॥

CHAPTER XV
THE WAY TO THE SUPREME PERSON

The Blessed Lord said :

1. They speak of the immutable Ashvattha tree with its root above and branches below, whose leaves are the Vedas ; he who knows it is a knower of the Vedas.

अधश्चोर्ध्वं प्रसृता-स्तस्य शाखा गुणप्रवृद्धा विषय-प्रवालाः।
अधश्च मूलान्यनुसंततानि कर्मानुबन्धीनि मनुष्यलोके ॥ २ ॥
न रूप-मस्येह तथोपलभ्यते नान्तो न चादिर्न च संप्रतिष्ठा।
अश्वत्थ-मेनं सुविरूढ-मूल-मसङ्ग-शस्त्रेण दृढेन छित्त्वा ॥ ३ ॥
ततः पदं तत् परिमार्गितव्यं यस्मिन् गता न निवर्तन्ति भूयः।
तमेव चाद्यं पुरुषं प्रपद्ये यतः प्रवृत्तिः प्रसृता पुराणी ॥ ४ ॥

2. Its branches, nurtured by the Gunas, spread below and above, its shoots are the sense-objects, and its rootlings are stretched below, producing actions in the world of men.

3-4. Its form as such is not experienced here, nor its end nor its beginning nor its continuity. Having severed this deeprooted Ashvattha tree with the strong weapon

SRIMAD-BHAGAVAD-GITA

निर्मानमोहा जित-सङ्गदोषा अध्यात्मनित्या विनिवृत्त-कामाः ।
द्वन्द्वै-र्विमुक्ताः सुखदुःखसंज्ञै-र्गच्छन्त्यमूढाः पद-मव्ययं तत्॥५॥
न तद्भासयते सूर्यो न शशाङ्को न पावकः ।
यद्गत्वा न निवर्तन्ते तद्धाम परमं मम ॥ ६ ॥

of non-attachment, one should next seek that goal reaching which they do not return, saying, "I seek refuge in that primordial Purusha from whom this eternal process has sprung."

5. Free from pride and delusion, over-coming the evil of attachment, ever devoted to spiritual pursuits, rid of desires and the dual throng named pleasure and pain, the wise go to that immutable goal.

6. The sun does not illumine it, nor the moon nor the fire; That is My Supreme State reaching which they do not return.

ममैवांशो जीवलोके जीवभूतः सनातनः ।
मनःषष्ठानीन्द्रियाणि प्रकृति-स्थानि कर्षति ॥ ७ ॥

शरीरं यदवाप्नोति यच्चाप्युत्क्रामतीश्वरः ।
गृहीत्वैतानि संयाति वायुर्गन्धानिवाशयात् ॥ ८ ॥

7. Verily, a part of Myself, having become this eternal embodied soul, draws to this world of beings the senses with the mind as the sixth, which rest in Nature (Prakriti).

8. When the master (soul) acquires a body, he takes these (the six referred to above) from the one he leaves, even as the breeze carries odours from their seats, and attains (the new body).

20

SRIMAD-BHAGAVAD-GITA

श्रोत्रं चक्षुः स्पर्शनं च रसनं घ्राणमेव च ।
अधिष्ठाय मनश्चायं विषया-नुपसेवते ॥ ९ ॥

उत्क्रामन्तं स्थितं वाऽपि भुञ्जानं वा गुणान्वितम् ।
विमूढा नानुपश्यन्ति पश्यन्ति ज्ञान-चक्षुषः ॥१०॥

9. Presiding over the ears, the eyes, the organs of touch, taste and smell, and also the mind, he enjoys the sense-objects.

10. The deluded do not see him departing (from this body) or residing (in it) or experiencing (objects), being associated with the senses; but they who have the eye of knowledge see him.

यतन्तो योगिनश्चैनं पश्यन्त्यात्मन्यवस्थितम् ।
यतन्तोऽप्यकृतात्मानो नैनं पश्यन्त्यचेतसः ॥ ११ ॥

यदादित्य-गतं तेजो जगद्भासयतेऽखिलम् ।
यच्चन्द्रमसि यच्चाग्नौ तत्तेजो विद्धि मामकम् ॥१२॥

11. The Yogis who strive see him seated in themselves, but those who are not self-controlled, being thoughtless, do not see him in spite of striving.

12. The light in the sun which illumines the world and that in the moon and the fire—know that light to be Mine.

SRIMAD-BHAGAVAD-GITA

गामाविश्य च भूतानि धारयाम्यहमोजसा ।
पुष्णामि चौषधीः सर्वाः सोमो भूत्वा रसात्मकः ॥ १३ ॥

अहं वैश्वानरो भूत्वा प्राणिनां देह-माश्रितः ।
प्राणापान-समायुक्तः पचाम्यन्नं चतु-र्विधम् ॥ १४ ॥

13. Entering the earth with My energy, I support the beings; and I nourish all the herbs, becoming the watery moon.

14. Residing in the bodies of beings as the digestive fire (Vaishvānara), and united with Prāna and Apāna (breaths), I digest the four kinds of food.

सर्वस्य चाहं हृदि सन्निविष्टो मत्तः स्मृति-ज्ञान-मपोहनं च ।
वेदैश्च सर्वै-रहमेव वेद्यो वेदान्तकृ-द्वेदविदेव चाहम् ॥ १५ ॥

द्वाविमौ पुरुषौ लोके क्षरश्चाक्षर एव च ।
क्षरः सर्वाणि भूतानि कूटस्थोऽक्षर उच्यते ॥ १६ ॥

15. I am seated in the heart of all beings; from Me are memory and knowledge as also their loss. I alone am to be known through all the Vedas, I am the originator of the Vedāntic tradition, and I am also the knower of the Vedas.

16. There are two beings (Purushas) in this world—perishable and imperishable; the perishable one is all these creatures, and the immutable is called the imperishable.

SRIMAD-BHAGAVAD-GITA

उत्तमः पुरुषस्त्वन्यः परमात्मेत्युदाहृतः ।
यो लोकत्रय-माविश्य बिभर्त्यव्यय ईश्वरः ॥ १७ ॥

यस्मात् क्षरमतीतोऽह-मक्षरादपि चोत्तमः ।
अतोऽस्मि लोके वेदे च प्रथितः पुरुषोत्तमः ॥१८॥

17. Different from these is the supreme Being known
as the supreme Self (Paramātman), the immutable Lord,
who having entered the three worlds sustains them.

18. Since I am beyond the perishable and even excel
the imperishable, therefore I am well known in this world
and in the Vedas as the supreme Being (Purushottama).

यो मामेवमसंमूढो जानाति पुरुषोत्तमम् ।
स सर्वविद्भजति मां सर्वभावेन भारत ॥ १९ ॥

इति गुह्यतमं शास्त्रमिदमुक्तं मयानघ ।
एतद्बुद्ध्वा बुद्धिमान्स्यात् कृतकृत्यश्च भारत ॥२०॥

इति श्रीमद्भगवद्गीतासूपनिषत्सु ब्रह्मविद्यायां योगशास्त्रे
श्रीकृष्णार्जुनसंवादे पुरुषोत्तमयोगो नाम
पञ्चदशोऽध्यायः ॥

19. He who, being thus undeluded, knows Me, the supreme Being, worships Me in all respects, O descendant of Bharata, and becomes all-knowing.

20. Thus this most secret doctrine has been expounded by Me, O sinless one. Knowing this, one becomes wise, and accomplished are all his duties, O descendant of Bharata.

॥ षोडशोऽध्यायः ॥
(दैवासुरसम्पद्विभागयोगः)

अभयं सत्त्वसंशुद्धि-र्ज्ञानयोग-व्यवस्थितिः ।
दानं दमश्च यज्ञश्च स्वाध्याय-स्तप आर्जवम् ॥ १ ॥

CHAPTER XVI
THE DISTINCTION BETWEEN DIVINE AND DEMONIAC ATTRIBUTES

The Blessed Lord said :

1. Fearlessness, purity of heart, steadfastness in the Yoga of knowledge, charity, self-control, sacrifice, study of the Vedas, austerity, uprightness.

DISTINCTION BETWEEN DIVINE AND DEMONIAC ATTRIBUTES

अहिंसा सत्य-मक्रोध-स्त्यागः शान्ति-रपैशुनम् ।
दया भूते-ष्वलोलुप्त्वं मार्देवं ह्री-रचापलम् ॥ २ ॥
तेजः क्षमा धृतिः शौच-मद्रोहो नातिमानिता ।
भवन्ति संपदं दैवी-मभिजातस्य भारत ॥ ३ ॥

2. Non-injury, truthfulness, absence of anger, self-sacrifice, tranquillity, freedom from slander, kindness to beings, non-covetousness, gentleness, modesty, absence of fickleness.

3. Boldness, forgiveness, fortitude, purity, absence of hatred, absence of conceit,—these belong to one born for divine wealth, O descendant of Bharata.

SRIMAD-BHAGAVAD-GITA

दम्भो दर्पोऽभिमानश्च क्रोधः पारुष्यमेव च ।
अज्ञानं चाभिजातस्य पार्थ संपद-मासुरीम् ॥ ४ ॥
दैवी संप-द्विमोक्षाय निबन्धायासुरी मता ।
मा शुचः संपदं दैवी-मभिजातोऽसि पाण्डव ॥ ५ ॥

4. Ostentation, arrogance, self-conceit, anger, rudeness, and ignorance belong, O Pārtha, to one who is born for demoniac wealth.

5. Divine wealth is deemed to lead to Liberation and the demoniac to bondage. Grieve not, O son of Pāndu, you are born for divine wealth.

द्वौ भूतसर्गौ लोकेऽस्मिन् दैव आसुर एव च।
दैवो विस्तरशः प्रोक्त आसुरं पार्थ मे शृणु ॥ ६ ॥

प्रवृत्तिं च निवृत्तिं च जना न विदुरासुराः।
न शौचं नापि चाचारो न सत्यं तेषु विद्यते ॥ ७ ॥

6. There are two types of beings created in this world—the divine and the demoniac. The divine type has been described at length; (now) hear from Me, O, Pārtha, of the demoniac.

7. Persons of a demoniac nature do not know what to do and what to refrain from; they have neither purity nor good conduct nor truth.

SRIMAD-BHAGAVAD-GITA

असत्य-मप्रतिष्ठं ते जगदाहु-रनीश्वरम् ।
अपरस्पर-संभूतं किमन्यत् कामहैतुकम् ॥ ८ ॥

एतां दृष्टि-मवष्टभ्य नष्टात्मानोऽल्पबुद्धयः ।
प्रभवन्त्युग्रकर्माणः क्षयाय जगतोऽहिताः ॥ ९ ॥

8. They describe the world as being without a truth,
without a basis, without a God and brought about by
mutual union—as nothing but originating in lust.

9. Holding this view, these ruined souls of small
intellects and of fierce deeds, are born for the destruction
of the world as its enemies.

काम-माश्रित्य दुष्पूरं दम्भ-मान-मदान्विताः ।
मोहाद्-गृहीत्वाऽसद्ग्राहान् प्रवर्तन्तेऽशुचिव्रताः॥१०॥
चिन्ता-मपरिमेयां च प्रलयान्ता-मुपाश्रिताः ।
कामोपभोगपरमा एतावदिति निश्चिताः ॥ ११ ॥

10. Resorting to insatiable desires, full of hypocrisy, pride and arrogance, they of impure vows act holding false views through delusion.

11. Beset with immense cares ending only with death, regarding gratification of sensual enjoyment as their highest aim, and convinced that this is all;

SRIMAD-BHAGAVAD-GITA

आशा-पाश-शतैर्बद्धाः काम-क्रोध परायणाः ।
ईहन्ते कामभोगार्थ-मन्यायेनार्थसञ्चयान् ॥ १२ ॥

इदमद्य मया लब्ध-मिमं प्राप्स्ये मनोरथम् ।
इदमस्तीदमपि मे भविष्यति पुनर्धनम् ॥ १३ ॥

12. Bound by a hundred ties of expectation and given
to lust and anger, they strive to collect by foul means hoards
of wealth for sense gratification.

13. "This has been gained to-day by me; this desire
I shall obtain; this wealth is mine, and this other too will
be mine.

असौ मया हतः शत्रु-र्हनिष्ये चापरानपि ।
ईश्वरोऽहं-महं भोगी सिद्धोऽहं बलवान् सुखी ॥ १४ ॥
आढ्योऽभिजनवा-नस्मि कोऽन्योऽस्ति सदृशो मया ।
यक्ष्ये दास्यामि मोदिष्य इत्यज्ञान-विमोहिताः ॥१५॥

14. "That enemy has been slain by me, and others too I will slay. I am the Lord, I am full of enjoyments, I am successful, powerful and happy.

15. "I am rich and of noble birth; who else is equal to me? I will sacrifice, I will make gifts, I will rejoice"- thus deluded by ignorance,

अनेकचित्त-विभ्रान्ता मोह-जाल-समावृताः ।
प्रसक्ताः कामभोगेषु पतन्ति नरकेऽशुचौ ॥ १६ ॥

आत्मसंभाविताः स्तब्धा धन-मान-मदान्विताः ।
यजन्ते नाम-यज्ञैस्ते दम्भेनाविधि-पूर्वकम् ॥ १७ ॥

16. Perplexed by many a fancy, entangled in the net of delusion, and addicted to the gratification of desires, they fall into foul hell.

17. Self-esteemed, arrogant, filled with vanity and haughtiness due to wealth, they ostentatiously perform sacrifices in name, disregarding prescribed methods.

DISTINCTION BETWEEN DIVINE AND DEMONIAC ATTRIBUTES

अहंकारं बलं दर्पं कामं क्रोधं च संश्रिताः ।
मामात्म-पर-देहेषु प्रद्विषन्तोऽभ्यसूयकाः ॥ १८ ॥

तानहं द्विषतः क्रूरान् संसारेषु नराधमान् ।
क्षिपाम्यजस्रमशुभानासुरीष्वेव योनिषु ॥ १९ ॥

18. Possessed of self-conceit, power, insolence, lust and anger, these cavilling people perform sacrifices, hating Me (residing) in their own bodies and in those of others.

19. These cruel haters, the most degraded of men, I hurl perpetually among demoniacal species in the transmigratory worlds.

SRIMAD-BHAGAVAD-GITA

आसुरीं योनि-मापन्ना मूढा जन्मनि जन्मनि ।
मामप्राप्यैव कौन्तेय ततो यान्त्यधमां गतिम् ॥ २० ॥

त्रिविधं नरकस्येदं द्वारं नाशन-मात्मनः ।
कामः क्रोध-स्तथा लोभ-स्तस्मादेतत्त्रयं त्यजेत्॥२१॥

20. Obtaining demoniac bodies, and deluded birth
after birth, far from attaining Me, O son of Kunti, they fall
into still lower conditions.

21. There are three types of gates to hell destructive of
the self—lust, anger and greed ; therefore these three should
be shunned.

एतैर्विमुक्तः कौन्तेय तमोद्वारैस्त्रिभिर्नरः ।
आचरत्यात्मनः श्रेयस्ततो याति परां गतिम् ॥२२॥

यः शास्त्रविधि-मुत्सृज्य वर्तते कामकारतः ।
न स सिद्धि-मवाप्नोति न सुखं न परां गतिम् ॥२३॥

22. The man who has got rid of these three gates to darkness, O son of Kunti, practises what is good for himself, and thus goes to the supreme Goal.

23. He who, setting aside the ordinances of the Scriptures, acts under the impulse of desire, attains neither perfection nor happiness nor the supreme Goal.

SRIMAD-BHAGAVAD-GITA

तस्मा-च्छास्त्रं प्रमाणं ते कार्याकार्य-व्यवस्थितौ ।
ज्ञात्वा शास्त्रविधानोक्तं कर्म कर्तु-मिहार्हसि ॥ २४ ॥

इति श्रीमद्भगवद्गीतासूपनिषत्सु ब्रह्मविद्यायां योगशास्त्रे
श्रीकृष्णार्जुनसंवादे दैवासुरसंपद्विभागयोगो नाम
षोडशोऽध्यायः ॥

24. So let the Scriptures be your authority in ascertaining what ought to be done and what ought not to be done. Having known what has been prescribed by the Scriptures, you should act in this matter.

॥ सप्तदशोऽध्यायः ॥

(श्रद्धात्रयविभागयोगः)

अर्जुन उवाच—
ये शास्त्रविधि-मुत्सृज्य यजन्ते श्रद्धयान्विताः ।
तेषां निष्ठा तु का कृष्ण सत्त्वमाहो रजस्तमः ॥ १ ॥

CHAPTER XVII

THE SEPARATION OF THE THREE KINDS OF FAITH

Arjuna said:

1. Those who setting aside the ordinances of the Scriptures perform sacrifices with faith (Shraddhā)—what is their status, O Krishna? Is it Sattva, or Rajas, or Tamas?

श्रीभगवानुवाच—

त्रिविधा भवति श्रद्धा देहिनां सा स्वभावजा ।
सात्त्विकी राजसी चैव तामसी चेति तां श्रृणु ॥ २ ॥

सत्त्वानुरूपा सर्वस्य श्रद्धा भवति भारत ।
श्रद्धा-मयोऽयं पुरुषो यो यच्छ्रद्धः स एव सः ॥ ३ ॥

The Blessed Lord said :

2. Threefold is the natural faith of embodied beings—
Sāttvika, Rājasika or Tāmasika.   Hear about it.

3. The faith of each person is according to his stuff,
O descendant of Bharata.   A man is made up of his faith :
he verily is what his faith is.

THE SEPARATION OF THE THREE KINDS OF FAITH

यजन्ते सात्त्विका देवान् यक्ष-रक्षांसि राजसाः ।
प्रेतान् भूतगणांश्चान्ये यजन्ते तामसा जनाः ॥ ४ ॥

अशास्त्र-विहितं घोरं तप्यन्ते ये तपो जनाः ।
दम्भाहङ्कार-संयुक्ताः काम-राग-बलान्विताः ॥ ५ ॥

कर्षयन्तः शरीरस्थं भूत-ग्राम-मचेतसः ।
मां चैवान्तः-शरीरस्थं तान्विद्ध्यासुर-निश्चयान् ॥ ६ ॥

4. The Sāttvika worship the gods, the Rājasika (worship) the Yakshas and Rākshasas, while others, the Tāmasika men, worship spirits and goblins.

5-6. Those men who practise severe austerities not enjoined by the Scriptures, being given to ostentation and

SRIMAD-BHAGAVAD-GITA

आहारस्त्वपि सर्वस्य त्रिविधो भवति प्रिग: ।

यज्ञ-स्तप-स्तथा दानं तेषां भेद-मिमं शृणु ॥ ७ ॥

आयु:-सत्त्व-बलारोग्य-सुख-प्रीति-विवर्धनाः ।

रस्याः स्निग्धाः स्थिरा हृद्या आहाराः सात्त्विक-प्रियाः ॥ ८ ॥

self-conceit, possessed of desire, attachment and pertinacity, and senseless, torture the elements in the body, as also Me residing within it—know them to be of demoniac resolves.

7. The food also liked by each is threefold, as also sacrifice, austerity and gift. Listen about these distinctions among them.

8. The foods that augment life, energy, strength, health, happiness and joy, and which are savoury, oleaginous, nourishing and agreeable, are liked by the Sāttvika.

कट्वम्ल-लवणात्युष्ण-तीक्ष्ण-रूक्ष-विदाहिनः ।
आहारा राजसस्येष्टा दुःख-शोकामय-प्रदाः ॥ ९ ॥

यात-यामं गतरसं पूति पर्युषितं च यत् ।
उच्छिष्टमपि चामेध्यं भोजनं तामस-प्रियम् ॥ १० ॥

9. The foods that are very bitter, sour, saltish, hot, pungent, dry and burning are liked by the Rājasika and are productive of pain, grief and disease.

10. The food that is pretty cold, worthless, putrid, stale, partly eaten and impure is liked by the Tāmasika.

318 SRIMAD-BHAGAVAD-GITA

अफलाकाङ्क्षिभि-र्यज्ञो विधि-दृष्टो य इज्यते ।
यष्टव्य-मेवेति मनः समाधाय स सात्त्विकः ॥ ११ ॥

अभिसंधाय तु फलं दम्भार्थमपि चैव यत् ।
इज्यते भरतश्रेष्ठ तं यज्ञं विद्धि राजसम् ॥ १२ ॥

11. That sacrifice which is performed according to scriptural injunctions by men desiring no fruit and with their mind fixed on it for its own sake is Sāttvika.

12. But know that sacrifice to be Rājasika, O best of the Bharatas, which is performed aiming at its fruit, as also for ostentation.

विधिहीन-मसृष्टान्नं मन्त्रहीन-मदक्षिणम् ।
श्रद्धा-विरहितं यज्ञं तामसं परिचक्षते ॥ १३ ॥

देव-द्विज-गुरु-प्राज्ञ-पूजनं शौच-मार्जवम् ।
ब्रह्मचर्य-महिंसा च शारीरं तप उच्यते ॥ १४ ॥

13. The sacrifice which is contrary to ordinance, in which no food is distributed, which is devoid of Mantras, gifts to the priests and faith, is said to be Tāmasika.

14. Worship of the gods, the twice-born, the preceptor and the wise, purity, straightforwardness, continence and non-injury, are said to be physical austerity.

SRIMAD-BHAGAVAD-GITA

अनुद्वेगकरं वाक्यं सत्यं प्रियहितं च यत् ।

स्वाध्यायाभ्यसनं चैव वाङ्मयं तप उच्यते ॥ १५ ॥

मनः-प्रसादः सौम्यत्वं मौन-मात्मविनिग्रहः ।

भावसंशुद्धि-रित्येत-चपो मानस-मुच्यते ॥ १६ ॥

15. Speech that causes no worry and is also truthful, agreeable and beneficial, as also study of the Vedas, are said to be verbal austerity.

16. Serenity of mind, kindliness, silence, self-control and purity of heart, are said to be mental austerity.

श्रद्धया परया तप्तं तपस्तत्त्रिविधं नरैः ।
अफलाकाङ्क्षिभिर्युक्तैः सात्त्विकं परिचक्षते ॥ १७ ॥

सत्कार-मान-पूजार्थं तपो दम्भेन चैव यत् ।
क्रियते तदिह प्रोक्तं राजसं चलमध्रुवम् ॥ १८ ॥

17. This threefold austerity practised with great faith by men who desire no fruit and are steadfast, is said to be Sāttvika.

18. That austerity which is practised to gain respect, honour and adoration, and that with ostentation, and which is transitory and unstable, is here said to be Rājasika.

SRIMAD-BHAGAVAD-GITA

मूढग्राहेणात्मनो यत्पीडया क्रियते तपः ।
परस्योत्सादनार्थं वा तत्तामस-मुदाहृतम् ॥ १९ ॥

दातव्यमिति यद्दानं दीयतेऽनुपकारिणे ।
देशे काले च पात्रे च तद्दानं सात्त्विकं स्मृतम् ॥ २० ॥

19. That austerity which is practised out of a foolish notion, with self-torture, or for the purpose of ruining another, is called Tāmasika.

20. To give is a duty—a gift given with this idea to one who will do no service in return, in a fit place and time and to a worthy person, is known to be Sāttvika.

यत्तु प्रत्युपकारार्थं फल-मुद्दिश्य वा पुनः ।
दीयते च परिक्लिष्टं तद्दानं राजसं स्मृतम् ॥ २१ ॥

अदेशकाले यद्दान-मपात्रेभ्यश्च दीयते ।
असत्कृत-मवज्ञातं तत्तामस-मुदाहृतम् ॥ २२ ॥

21. That gift, however, which is given with a view to receiving in return, or looking for its fruit, or grudgingly, is said to be Rājasika.

22. The gift that is given at the wrong place and time and to unworthy persons, without regard and disdainfully, is said to be Tāmasika.

SRIMAD-BHAGAVAD-GITA

ओं तत्सदिति निर्देशो ब्रह्मण-स्त्रिविधः स्मृतः ।
ब्राह्मणा-स्तेन वेदाश्च यज्ञाश्च विहिताः पुरा ॥ २३ ॥
तस्मा-दोमित्युदाहृत्य यज्ञ-दान-तपः-क्रियाः ।
प्रवर्तन्ते विधानोक्ताः सततं ब्रह्मवादिनाम् ॥ २४ ॥

23. 'Om Tat Sat'—this is considered to be the three-fold designation of Brahman. By that were fashioned, of old, the Brāhmanas, the Vedas and sacrifices.

24. Therefore the acts of sacrifice, gift and austerity enjoined by the ordinance, on the part of the followers of the Vedas, by uttering the word 'Om', are always begun well.

तदित्यनभिसंधाय फलं यज्ञतपः-क्रियाः ।
दान-क्रियाश्च विविधाः क्रियन्ते मोक्ष-काङ्क्षिभिः ॥ २५ ॥

सद्भावे साधु-भावे च सदित्येतत् प्रयुज्यते ।
प्रशस्ते कर्मणि तथा सच्छब्दः पार्थ युज्यते ॥ २६ ॥

25. Uttering 'Tat', the various acts of sacrifice, austerity and charity are performed by the seekers of Liberation without aiming at their fruit.

26. 'Sat' is used to denote existence and goodness; so also, O Pārtha, the word 'Sat' is used for any auspicious act.

यज्ञे तपसि दाने च स्थितिः सदिति चोच्यते ।
कर्म चैव तदर्थीयं सदित्येवाभिधीयते ॥ २७ ॥

अश्रद्धया हुतं दत्तं तपस्तप्तं कृतं च यत् ।
असदित्युच्यते पार्थ न च तत्प्रेत्य नो इह ॥ २८ ॥

इति श्रीमद्भगवद्गीतासूपनिषत्सु ब्रह्मविद्यायां योगशास्त्रे
श्रीकृष्णार्जुनसंवादे श्रद्धात्रयविभागयोगो नाम
सप्तदशोऽध्यायः ॥

27. Steadiness in sacrifice, austerity and gift is also called 'Sat'; as also work even done indirectly for the sake of the Lord is verily called 'Sat'.

28. Offering oblations, making gifts, austerities practised, or anything else done—without faith, are called 'Asat' O Pārtha; they fructify neither hereafter nor here.

॥ अष्टादशोऽध्यायः ॥

(मोक्षसन्न्यासयोगः)

अर्जुन उवाच—
सन्न्यासस्य महाबाहो तत्त्व-मिच्छामि वेदितुम् ।
त्यागस्य च हृषीकेश पृथ-केशिनिषूदन ॥ १ ॥

CHAPTER XVIII
THE WAY OF RENUNCIATION

Arjuna said:

1. I desire to know distinctly the true nature of renunciation (Sannyāsa), O Hrishikesa, as also of relinquishment (Tyāga), O mighty-armed One, O slayer of Keshin.

SRIMAD-BHAGAVAD-GITA

श्री भगवानुवाच—

काम्यानां कर्मणां न्यासं सन्न्यासं कवयो विदुः ।
सर्वकर्म-फलत्यागं प्राहुस्त्यागं विचक्षणाः ॥ २ ॥

त्याज्यं दोषव-दित्येके कर्म प्राहु-र्मनीषिणः ।
यज्ञ-दान-तपः कर्म न त्याज्य-मिति चापरे ॥ ३ ॥

The Blessed Lord Said :

2: Sages understand the renouncing of actions that fulfil desires as renunciation (Sannyāsa) and the learned declare the abandoning of the fruit of all actions as relinquishment (Tyāga).

3: Some philosophers declare that all action should be relinquished as being evil, while others say that the work in the form of sacrifice, gift and austerity should not be relinquished.

निश्चयं शृणु मे तत्र त्यागे भरतसत्तम ।
त्यागो हि पुरुषव्याघ्र त्रिविधः संप्रकीर्तितः ॥ ४ ॥

यज्ञ-दान-तपः कर्म न त्याज्यं कार्यमेव तत् ।
यज्ञो दानं तपश्चैव पावनानि मनीषिणाम् ॥ ५ ॥

4. Hear from Me the final truth about this relinquishment, O best of the Bharatas; for relinquishment is truly declared to be of three kinds, O best of men.

5. Work in the form of sacrifice, gift and austerity should not be relinquished, but should indeed be performed; (for) sacrifice, gift and austerity are sanctifying to the wise.

SRIMAD-BHAGAVAD-GITA

एतान्यपि तु कर्माणि सङ्गं त्यक्त्वा फलानि च ।
कर्तव्यानीति मे पार्थ निश्चितं मतमुत्तमम् ॥ ६ ॥

नियतस्य तु सन्न्यासः कर्मणो नोपपद्यते ।
मोहात् तस्य परित्याग-स्तामसः परिकीर्तितः ॥ ७ ॥

6. But even these activities should be performed giving up attachment and fruit—this is My decided and best view.

7. But the renunciation of obligatory work is not proper; abandonment of such work from delusion is declared to be Tāmasika.

दुःखमित्येव यत्कर्म कायक्लेश-भयात् त्यजेत् ।
स कृत्वा राजसं त्यागं नैव त्यागफलं लभेत् ॥ ८ ॥

कार्यमित्येव यत्कर्म नियतं क्रियतेऽर्जुन ।
सङ्गं त्यक्त्वा फलं चैव स त्यागः सात्त्विको मतः ॥ ९ ॥

8. If from fear of bodily trouble, one relinquishes action because it is irksome, thus performing a Rājasika relinquishment, one certainly does not obtain the fruit of relinquishment.

9. When obligatory work is performed, O Arjuna, only because it ought to be done, giving up attachment for it and its fruit—that relinquishment is regarded as Sāttvika

SRIMAD-BHAGAVAD-GITA

न द्वेष्ट्यकुशलं कर्म कुशले नानुषज्जते ।
त्यागी सत्त्व-समाविष्टो मेधावी छिन्नसंशयः ॥ १० ॥

न हि देहभृता शक्यं त्यक्तुं कर्मा-ण्यशेषतः ।
यस्तु कर्मफलत्यागी स त्यागी-त्यभिधीयते ॥ ११ ॥

10. The relinquisher endued with Sattva and a steady understanding, having his doubts resolved, neither hates disagreeable work nor is attached to agreeable work.

11. Action cannot be entirely relinquished by an embodied being. He who relinquishes the fruit of action, is called a relinquisher.

अनिष्टमिष्टं मिश्रं च त्रिविधं कर्मणः फलम् ।
भवत्यत्यागिनां प्रेत्य न तु सन्न्यासिनां क्वचित् ॥ १२ ॥
पञ्चैतानि महाबाहो कारणानि निबोध मे ।
सांख्ये कृतान्ते प्रोक्तानि सिद्धये सर्वकर्मणाम् ॥ १३ ॥

12. The threefold fruit of action—disagreeable, agreeable and mixed—accrues to non-relinquishers after death, but never to relinquishers.

13. Learn from Me, O mighty-armed one, these five causes for the accomplishment of all work, as declared in the wisdom which is the end of all action.

SRIMAD-BHAGAVAD-GITA

अधिष्ठानं तथा कर्ता करणं च पृथग्विधम् ।
विविधाश्च पृथक्चेष्टा दैवं चैवात्र पञ्चमम् ॥ १४ ॥

शरीर-वाङ्मनोभि-र्यत्कर्म प्रारभते नरः ।
न्याय्यं वा विपरीतं वा पञ्चैते तस्य हेतवः ॥ १५ ॥

14. The seat of action and likewise the agent, the various senses, the different and manifold efforts—the presiding divinity being the fifth of these.

15. Whatever action a man performs by his body, speech and mind, whether proper or the reverse, has these five as its causes.

तत्रैवं सति कर्तार-मात्मानं केवलं तु यः ।
पश्य-त्यकृतबुद्धित्वान्न स पश्यति दुर्मतिः ॥ १६ ॥
यस्य नाहंकृतो भावो बुद्धि-र्यस्य न लिप्यते ।
हत्वापि स इमाँ-ल्लोकान्न हन्ति न निबध्यते ॥ १७ ॥

16. Such being the case, he who owing to his unrefined understanding looks upon the Absolute Self as the agent, is foolish, and does not see.

17. He who is free from the notion of 'I' (egoism), and whose understanding is not trammelled, though he kills these beings, does not really kill, nor is he bound.

SRIMAD-BHAGAVAD-GITA

ज्ञानं ज्ञेयं परिज्ञाता त्रिविधा कर्म-चोदना ।
करणं कर्म कर्तेति त्रिविधः कर्म-संग्रहः ॥ १८ ॥

ज्ञानं कर्म च कर्ता च त्रिधैव गुण-भेदतः ।
प्रोच्यते गुण-संख्याने यथाव-च्छृणु तान्यपि ॥ १९ ॥

18.   Knowledge, the knowable and the knower form the threefold impulse to action.   The instrument, the object and the agent form the threefold basis of action.

19.   Knowledge, action and agent are declared in the science of the Gunas to be of three kinds only, according to the distinction of the Gunas ; of them also hear duly.

सर्वभूतेषु येनैकं भावमव्ययमीक्षते ।
अविभक्तं विभक्तेषु तज्ज्ञानं विद्धि सात्त्विकम् ॥ २० ॥

पृथक्त्वेन तु यज्ज्ञानं नानाभावान्पृथग्विधान् ।
वेत्ति सर्वेषु भूतेषु तज्ज्ञानं विद्धि राजसम् ॥ २१ ॥

20. The knowledge by which one sees the one undivided, imperishable substance in all beings which are divided, should be known to be Sāttvika.

21. But the knowledge by which one sees as distinct, in all beings, different entities of various kinds, should be known to be Rājasika.

SRIMAD-BHAGAVAD-GITA

यत्तु कृत्स्नव-देकस्मिन् कार्ये सक्त-महैतुकम् ।
अतत्त्वार्थव-दल्पं च तत्तामस-मुदाहृतम् ॥ २२ ॥

नियतं सङ्गरहित-मरागद्वेषतः कृतम् ।
अफल-प्रेप्सुना कर्म यत्तत्सात्त्विक-मुच्यते ॥ २३ ॥

22. Whilst that knowledge which is confined to a
single product as if it were the whole, which is irrational,
not founded upon truth, and trivial, is declared to be
Tāmasika.

23. An action that is ordained, performed without
attachment, free from attraction or repulsion, by one not
coveting its fruit, is declared to be Sāttvika.

यत्तु कामेप्सुना कर्म साहंकारेण वा पुनः ।
क्रियते बहुलायासं तद्राजस-मुदाहृतम् ॥ २४ ॥

अनुबन्धं क्षयं हिंसा-मनपेक्ष्य च पौरुषम् ।
मोहा-दारभ्यते कर्म यत्तत्तामस-मुच्यते ॥ २५ ॥

24. But an action that is done by a person seeking desire or possessed of conceit, and that with much trouble, is declared to be Rājasika.

25. That action which is undertaken through delusion, without regard to consequence, loss, hurtfulness and capacity, is declared to be Tāmasika.

SRIMAD-BHAGAVAD-GITA

मुक्तसङ्गो-ऽनहंवादी धृत्युत्साह-समन्वितः ।
सिद्ध्यसिद्ध्यो-र्निर्विकारः कर्ता सात्त्विक उच्यते ॥ २६ ॥

रागी कर्मफल-प्रेप्सु-र्लुब्धो हिंसात्मकोऽशुचिः ।
हर्षशोकान्वितः कर्ता राजसः परिकीर्तितः ॥ २७ ॥

26. An agent who is free from attachment, non-egoistic, endued with fortitude and enthusiasm, and unaffected by success or failure, is called Sāttvika.

27. An agent who is interested, desirous of the fruit of action, greedy, malevolent, unclean and subject to elation and dejection, is declared to be Rājasika.

अयुक्तः प्राकृतः स्तब्धः शठो नैष्कृतिकोऽलसः ।
विषादी दीर्घसूत्री च कर्ता तामस उच्यते ॥ २८ ॥

बुद्धे-र्भेदं धृतेश्चैव गुणत-स्त्रिविधं शृणु ।
प्रोच्यमान-मशेषेण पृथक्त्वेन धनञ्जय ॥ २९ ॥

28. An agent who is unsteady, vulgar, arrogant, deceptive, overbearing, indolent, despondent and procrastinating, is said to be Tāmasika.

29. Listen now to the threefold variety, according to the Gunas, of the understanding and tenacity, as I declare them exhaustively and severally, O Dhananjaya.

SRIMAD-BHAGAVAD-GITA

प्रवृत्ति च निवृत्ति च कार्याकार्ये भयाभये ।
बन्धं मोक्षं च या वेत्ति बुद्धिः सा पार्थ सात्त्विकी ॥ ३० ॥
यया धर्म-मधर्मं च कार्यं चाकार्यमेव च ।
अयथावत्प्रजानाति बुद्धिः सा पार्थ राजसी ॥ ३१ ॥

30. That understanding which knows inclination and abstention, what ought to be done and what ought not to be done, fear and absence of fear, and bondage and Liberation, is Sāttvika, O Pārtha.

31. That understanding by which one knows incorrectly righteousness and unrighteousness, and what ought to be done and what ought not to be done, is Rājasika, O Pārtha.

अधर्मं धर्ममिति या मन्यते तमसावृता ।
सर्वार्थान् विपरीतांश्च बुद्धिः सा पार्थ तामसी ॥ ३२ ॥

धृत्या यया धारयते मनः-प्राणेन्द्रिय-क्रियाः ।
योगेनाव्यभिचारिण्या धृतिः सा पार्थ सात्त्विकी ॥ ३३ ॥

32. That understanding which, enveloped in ignorance, regards unrighteousness as righteousness and all things in an inverted way, is Tāmasika, O Pārtha.

33. That tenacity, unswerving through Yoga, by which one controls the functions of the mind, the breaths (Prānas) and the senses, is Sāttvika, O Pārtha.

SRIMAD-BHAGAVAD-GITA

यया तु धर्म-कामार्थान् धृत्या धारयतेऽर्जुन ।

असङ्गेन फलाकाङ्क्षी धृतिः सा पार्थ राजसी ॥ ३४ ॥

यया स्वप्नं भयं शोकं विषादं मदमेव च ।

न विमुञ्चति दुर्मेधा धृतिः सा पार्थ तामसी ॥ ३५ ॥

34. But the tenacity by which one holds fast to duty, pleasure and wealth, desiring their fruit because of attachment, is Rajasika, O Pārtha.

35. But the tenacity by which a stupid person does not give up sleep, fear, grief, depression and pride, is Tāmasika, O Pārtha.

सुखं त्विदानीं त्रिविधं शृणु मे भरतर्षभ ।
अभ्यासाद्रमते यत्र दुःखान्तं च निगच्छति ॥ ३६ ॥

यत्तदग्रे विषमिव परिणामेऽमृतोपमम् ।
तत्सुखं सात्त्विकं प्रोक्त-मात्म-बुद्धि-प्रसादजम् ॥ ३७ ॥

36-37. Now hear from Me, O Prince among the Bharatas, of the threefold happiness: The happiness which one relishes through practice, in which one comes to the end of all pain, and which is like poison at first, but like nectar at the end, is declared to be Sāttvika, born of the serenity of the understanding that concerns itself with the Self.

SRIMAD-BHAGAVAD-GITA

विषयेन्द्रिय-संयोगा-द्यत्तदग्रेऽमृतोपमम् ।
परिणामे विषमिव तत्सुखं राजसं स्मृतम् ॥ ३८ ॥

यदग्रे चानुबन्धे च सुखं मोहन-मात्मनः ।
निद्रालस्य-प्रमादोत्थं तत्तामस-मुदाहृतम् ॥ ३९ ॥

38. The happiness that arises from a contact between the objects and the senses, which is like nectar at the beginning, but like poison at the end, is said to be Rājasika.

39. That happiness which is self-delusive both at the beginning and at the end, and which arises from sleep, lassitude and inadvertence, is said to be Tāmasika.

न तदस्ति पृथिव्यां वा दिवि देवेषु वा पुनः ।
सत्त्वं प्रकृतिजैर्मुक्तं यदेभिः स्यात्त्रिभिर्गुणैः ॥ ४० ॥

ब्राह्मण-क्षत्रिय-विशां शूद्राणां च परंतप ।
कर्माणि प्रविभक्तानि स्वभाव-प्रभवैर्गुणैः ॥ ४१ ॥

40. There is no being on earth or again in heaven among the gods, that is free from these three Gunas born of Nature.

41. The duties of the Brāhmanas, Kshatriyas and Vaishyas, as also of the Sudras, are clearly divided, O scorcher of foes, according to the dispositions born of their own nature.

SRIMAD-BHAGAVAD-GITA

शमो दमस्तपः शौचं क्षान्ति-रार्जवमेव च ।
ज्ञानं विज्ञान-मास्तिक्यं ब्रह्मकर्म स्वभावजम् ॥ ४२ ॥

शौर्यं तेजो धृति-दाक्ष्यं युद्धे चाप्यपलायनम् ।
दान-मीश्वरभावश्च क्षात्रं कर्म स्वभावजम् ॥ ४३ ॥

42. Serenity, self-control, austerity, purity, forbea-rance, and also uprightness, knowledge, realization and faith, are the duties of a Brāhmana born of his nature.

43. Heroism, boldness, firmness, dexterity, not fleeing from the battle, generosity and lordliness, are the duties of a Kshatriya born of his nature.

कृषि-गौरक्ष्य-वाणिज्यं वैश्य-कर्म स्वभावजम् ।
परिचर्यात्मकं कर्म शूद्रस्यापि स्वभावजम् ॥ ४४ ॥
स्वे स्वे कर्म-ण्यभिरतः संसिद्धिं लभते नरः ।
स्वकर्म-निरतः सिद्धिं यथा विन्दति तच्छृणु ॥ ४५ ॥

44. Agriculture, cattle-rearing and trade are the duties of a Vaishya born of his nature; and work of the nature of service is the duty of a Sudra born of his nature.

45. Devoted to his own duty, a man attains perfection. Listen how one engaged in one's own duty attains perfection.

यतः प्रवृत्ति-भूतानां येन सर्वमिदं ततम् ।
स्वकर्मणा तमभ्यर्च्य सिद्धिं विन्दति मानवः ॥ ४६ ॥

श्रेयान् स्वधर्मो विगुणः परधर्मात् स्वनुष्ठितात् ।
स्वभाव-नियतं कर्म कुर्व-न्नाप्नोति किल्बिषम् ॥ ४७ ॥

46. From whom proceeds the activity of all beings, and by whom all this is pervaded—worshipping Him through his own duty a man attains perfection.

47. Better is one's own duty, though defective, than the duty of another, well performed. Doing the duty ordained by one's own nature, one incurs no sin.

सहजं कर्म कौन्तेय सदोषमपि न त्यजेत् ।
सर्वारम्भा हि दोषेण धूमेनाग्नि-रिवावृताः ॥ ४८ ॥

असक्त-बुद्धिः सर्वत्र जितात्मा विगतस्पृहः ।
नैष्कर्म्यसिद्धिं परमां सन्न्यासेनाधिगच्छति ॥ ४९ ॥

48. One should not, O son of Kunti, relinquish the duty to which one is born, although it may be attended with evil; for all undertakings are covered by defect, as fire by smoke.

49. He, whose understanding is unattached everywhere, whose mind is conquered, who is bereft of desires, attains by renunciation that supreme state of freedom from action.

SRIMAD-BHAGAVAD-GITA

सिद्धिं प्राप्तो यथा ब्रह्म तथाप्नोति निबोध मे ।
समासेनैव कौन्तेय निष्ठा ज्ञानस्य या परा ॥ ५० ॥

बुद्ध्या विशुद्धया युक्तो धृत्यात्मानं नियम्य च ।
शब्दादीन् विषयांस्त्यक्त्वा रागद्वेषौ व्युदस्य च ॥ ५१ ॥

50. Learn from Me in brief, O son of Kunti, how reaching (such) perfection he attains Brahman, which is the supreme consummation of knowledge.

51. Endued with a pure understanding, controlling the mind with tenacity, relinquishing sense-objects such as sound, and laying aside likes and dislikes,

विविक्त-सेवी लघ्वाशी यतवाकाय-मानसः ।
ध्यानयोग-परो नित्यं वैराग्यं समुपाश्रितः ॥ ५२ ॥

अहङ्कारं बलं दर्पं कामं क्रोधं परिग्रहम् ।
विमुच्य निर्ममः शान्तो ब्रह्मभूयाय कल्पते ॥ ५३ ॥

52. Resorting to a sequestered place, eating little, controlled in speech, body and mind, always devoted to the Yoga of contemplation, cultivating dispassion,

53. Forsaking egotism, power, arrogance, desire, anger and superfluous things, free from the notion of 'mine' and tranquil, he is fit for becoming Brahman.

SRIMAD-BHAGAVAD-GITA

ब्रह्मभूतः प्रसन्नात्मा न शोचति न काङ्क्षति ।
समः सर्वेषु भूतेषु मद्भक्तिं लभते पराम् ॥ ५४ ॥

भक्त्या मामभिजानाति यावान् यश्चास्मि तत्त्वतः ।
ततो मां तत्त्वतो ज्ञात्वा विशते तदनन्तरम् ॥ ५५ ॥

54. Becoming Brahman and tranquil-minded, he neither grieves nor desires ; alike to all beings, he attains supreme devotion to Me.

55. By devotion he knows Me truly, how much and what I am. Then, having known Me truly, he forthwith enters into Me.

सर्वकर्माण्यपि सदा कुर्वाणो मद्व्यपाश्रयः ।
मत्प्रसादा-दवाप्नोति शाश्वतं पदमव्ययम् ॥ ५६ ॥

चेतसा सर्वकर्माणि मयि सन्न्यस्य मत्परः ।
बुद्धियोग-मुपाश्रित्य मच्चित्तः सततं भव ॥ ५७ ॥

56. Even performing all works always, taking refuge in Me, he attains through My grace the eternal and immutable state.

57. Resigning mentally all actions to Me, regarding Me as the supreme goal, and resorting to Yoga through the intellect, ever fix your mind on Me.

SRIMAD-BHAGAVAD-GITA

मच्चित्तः सर्वदुर्गाणि मत्प्रसादा-चरिष्यसि ।
अथ चेत्त्वमहङ्कारान्न श्रोष्यसि विनङ्क्ष्यसि ॥ ५८ ॥

यदहङ्कार-माश्रित्य न योत्स्य इति मन्यसे ।
मिथ्यैष व्यवसायस्ते प्रकृतिस्त्वां नियोक्ष्यति ॥ ५९ ॥

58. Fixing your mind on Me, you will overcome all
difficulties through My grace. But if from self-conceit you
do not listen to Me, you will perish.

59. That, indulging in self-conceit, you think, 'I will
not fight'—vain is this resolve of yours. Your nature will
compel you (to fight).

स्वभावजेन कौन्तेय निबद्धः स्वेन कर्मणा ।
कर्तुं नेच्छसि यन्मोहात् करिष्यस्यवशोऽपि तत् ॥ ६० ॥

ईश्वरः सर्वभूतानां हृद्देशेऽर्जुन तिष्ठति ।
भ्रामयन् सर्वभूतानि यन्त्रारूढानि मायया ॥ ६१ ॥

60. O son of Kunti, what you out of delusion do not wish to do, you shall do in spite of yourself, fettered by your own duty born of your nature.

61. In the heart of all beings, O Arjuna, resides the Lord, whirling all of them by His Māyā as if they were mounted on a machine.

SRIMAD-BHAGAVAD-GITA

तमेव शरणं गच्छ सर्वभावेन भारत ।

तत्प्रसादात् परां शान्तिं स्थानं प्राप्स्यसि शाश्वतम् ॥ ६२ ॥

इति ते ज्ञान-माख्यातं गुह्याद्-गुह्यतरं मया ।

विमृश्यैतद्-अशेषेण यथेच्छसि तथा कुरु ॥ ६३ ॥

62. Take refuge in Him alone with all your heart,
O descendant of Bharata (Arjuna); by His grace you shall
attain supreme peace and the eternal abode.

63. Thus has knowledge, more secret than all secrets,
been declared to you by Me; reflect on it fully and act as
you like.

सर्वगुह्यतमं भूयः शृणु मे परमं वचः ।
इष्टोऽसि मे दृढमिति ततो वक्ष्यामि ते हितम् ॥ ६४ ॥

मन्मना भव मद्भक्तो मद्याजी मां नमस्कुरु ।
मामेवैष्यसि सत्यं ते प्रतिजाने प्रियोऽसि मे ॥ ६५ ॥

64. Hear again My supreme word, the most secret of all. Because you are dearly beloved of Me, therefore I shall tell you what is good for you.

65. Fix your mind on Me, be devoted to Me, worship Me, and bow down to Me; then you shall come to Me. Truly do I promise to you, for you are dear to Me.

SRIMAD-BHAGAVAD-GITA

सर्वधर्मान् परित्यज्य मामेकं शरणं व्रज ।
अहं त्वा सर्वपापेभ्यो मोक्षयिष्यामि मा शुचः ॥ ६६ ॥

इदं ते नातपस्काय नाभक्ताय कदाचन ।
न चाशुश्रूषवे वाच्यं न च मां योऽभ्यसूयति ॥ ६७ ॥

66. Giving up all duties, take refuge in Me alone.
I will liberate you from all sins, do not grieve.

67. Never should this be declared by you to one who
is devoid of austerities, or who is not a devotee, nor to one
who does not wish to hear it, nor one who cavils at Me.

THE WAY OF RENUNCIATION

य इमं परमं गुह्यं मद्भक्तेष्वभिधास्यति ।
भक्तिं मयि परां कृत्वा मामेवैष्य-त्यसंशयः ॥ ६८ ॥

न च तस्मान्मनुष्येषु कश्चिन्मे प्रियकृत्तमः ।
भविता न च मे तस्मा-दन्यः प्रियतरो भुवि ॥ ६९ ॥

68. He who will impart this profound secret to My devotees, has supreme devotion to Me, and being free from doubt comes to Me alone.

69. There is none among men who does dearer service to Me than he, nor will there be any; and there is none on earth dearer to Me than he.

SRIMAD-BHAGAVAD-GITA

अध्येष्यते च य इमं धर्म्यं संवाद-मावयोः ।

ज्ञानयज्ञेन तेनाह-मिष्टः स्यामिति मे मतिः ॥ ७० ॥

श्रद्धावा-ननसूयश्च शृणुयादपि यो नरः ।

सोऽपि मुक्तः शुभाँल्लोकान् प्राप्नुयात् पुण्यकर्मणाम् ॥ ७१ ॥

70. And he who will study this sacred dialogue between us, will be sacrificing to Me through the knowledge-sacrifice; this is My opinion.

71. A person who merely hears (the Gita) with devotion and without cavilling shall be freed and attain the blessed spheres attained by men of righteous deeds.

कच्चिदेतच्छ्रुतं पार्थ त्वयैकाग्रेण चेतसा ।
कच्चिद्-अज्ञान-संमोहः प्रणष्टस्ते धनञ्जय ॥ ७२ ॥
अर्जुन उवाच—
नष्टो मोहः स्मृति-लब्धा त्वत्प्रसादान्मयाच्युत ।
स्थितोऽस्मि गतसन्देहः करिष्ये वचनं तव ॥ ७३ ॥

72. Have you listened to it, O Pārtha, with undivided attention? Has your delusion due to ignorance been destroyed, O Dhananjaya?

Arjuna said:

73. My delusion is destroyed, and I have gained my memory, through Your grace, O Achyuta. I stand free from doubt. I will carry out Your behest.

SRIMAD-BHAGAVAD-GITA

सञ्जय उवाच—

इत्यहं वासुदेवस्य पार्थस्य च महात्मनः ।
संवाद-मिम-मश्रौष-मद्भुतं रोमहर्षणम् ॥ ७४ ॥

व्यासप्रसादा-च्छ्रुतवा-नेतद्-गुह्यमहं परम् ।
योगं योगेश्वरात् कृष्णात् साक्षात् कथयतः स्वयम् ॥ ७५ ॥

Sanjaya said :

74. Thus have I heard this wonderful dialogue between Vāsudeva and the high-souled Pārtha, that causes my hair to stand on end.

75. Through the grace of Vyāsa I have heard this supreme and secret Yoga direct from Sri Krishna, the Lord of Yoga, as He declared it Himself.

राजन् संस्मृत्य संस्मृत्य संवाद-मिम-मद्भुतम् ।
केशवार्जुनयोः पुण्यं हृष्यामि च मुहुर्मुहुः ॥७६॥

तच्च संस्मृत्य संस्मृत्य रूप-मत्यद्भुतं हरेः ।
विस्मयो मे महान् राजन् हृष्यामि च पुनःपुनः ॥७७॥

76. O king, recalling often this wonderful and sacred dialogue between Keshava and Arjuna, I rejoice again and again.

77. And as I repeatedly recall that most wonderful form of Hari, great is my wonder, O king, and I rejoice again and again.

SRIMAD-BHAGAVAD-GITA

यत्र योगेश्वरः कृष्णो यत्र पार्थो धनुर्धरः ।
तत्र श्री-विजयो भूति-ध्रुवा नीति-र्मतिर्मम ॥७८॥

इति श्रीमहाभारते शतसाहस्र्यां संहितायां वैयासिक्यां भीष्म
पर्वणि श्रीमद्भगवद्गीतासूपनिषत्सु ब्रह्मविद्यायां योगशास्त्रे
श्रीकृष्णार्जुनसंवादे मोक्षसन्न्यासयोगो नाम
अष्टादशोऽध्यायः ॥

78. Where there is Sri Krishna, the Lord of Yoga, and where there is Pārtha, the wielder of the bow, there are sure fortune, victory, prosperity and statesmanship. Such is my conviction.

GREATNESS OF THE GITA

गीताशास्त्रमिदं पुण्यं यः पठेत्प्रयतः पुमान् ।
विष्णोः पदमवाप्नोति भयशोकादिवर्जितः ॥ १ ॥

1. He who diligently reads this sacred scripture, the Gita, becomes free from fear and sorrow, and attains the region of Sri Mahā Vishnu

गीताध्ययनशीलस्य प्राणायामपरस्य च ।
नैव सन्ति हि पापानि पूर्वजन्मकृतानि च ॥ २ ॥

2. For him who is in the habit of studying the Gītā and doing Prāṇāyāmā, there are no sins even of previous births.

GREATNESS OF THE GITA

मलनिर्मोचनं पुंसां जलस्नानं दिने दिने ।
सकृद्‍गीताम्भसि स्नानं संसारमलनाशनम् ॥ ३ ॥

3. Daily baths in water cleanse men externally, but a single bath in the waters of the Gita removes the taint of Samsāra (cycle of transmigration).

गीता सुगीता कर्तव्या किमन्यैः शास्त्रविस्तरैः ।
या स्वयं पद्मनाभस्य मुखपद्माद्विनिःसृता ॥ ४ ॥

4. Why go in for other elaborate scriptures, when you can chant the Gita which has issued from the lotus mouth of Padmanābha (Sri Mahā Vishnu) Himself?

भारतामृतसर्वस्वं विष्णोर्वक्त्राद्विनिःसृतम् ।
गीतागङ्गोदकं पीत्वा पुनर्जन्म न विद्यते ॥ ५ ॥

5. There is no rebirth for one after drinking the waters of the Gītā-Ganga which has flowed out of the mouth of Sri Mahā Vishnu and which is the quintessence of the nectar that is Mahabhārata.

एकं शास्त्रं देवकीपुत्रगीतमेको देवो देवकीपुत्र एव ।
एको मन्त्रस्तस्य नामानि यानि कर्माप्येकं तस्य देवस्य सेवा॥६॥

6. The song of the son of Devaki (Krishna) is the one scripture; the son of Devaki is the one God; His names form the one Mantra; and service of Him constitutes the only duty.